Same Today

GEORGE CRABB

The Same Today

Copyright © 2016 George Crabb

All rights reserved.

ISBN: 1523221283
ISBN-13: 978-1523221288

Scripture taken from the New King James Version. Copyright 1982 by Thomas Nelson, Inc. Used by permission. All rights reserved.

Cover: Water color painting of the point by the author.

Some of the names in this book have been changed for privacy and security reasons.

DEDICATION

Dedicated to all who are thirsty for the truth of why we are here. The truth is...

The Same Today

CONTENTS

Chapter One: The Perfect Day 1
Chapter Two: Seeds to Life 23
Chapter Three: Surfing the World 39
Chapter Four: Ranger 69
Chapter Five: Grace 127
Chapter Six: The Return 153
Chapter Seven: The Same Today 167
About the Author 195
Other Books by the Author 199

ACKNOWLEDGMENTS

It's by God's amazing grace that I am able to write this book. I would like to thank my lovely wife for her love, her unconditional love. I thank my father and mother for their help in writing this book. I thank all of my fellow Rangers and acknowledge their selfless service and sacrifice.

Chapter One: The Perfect day

Every winter huge storms off of the Pacific would wash sand down the reefs and point breaks in Santa Cruz. When this happened the rocky reef at the point was filled in with sand from 38th Avenue all the way down to the Hook. So the surf created by these natural elements, combined to form a wave of perfection.

It was a sunny winter afternoon in 1987 and I remember my high school friends were already out. The wind was slightly off shore, the ground swell was from a perfect direction at seven feet and the "38th Avenue sandbar built up perfectly. I remember surfing down from First Peak to 38th Avenue which was the same size. The high velocity of speed reached while surfing these special waves was like no other.

My surfing was on this day and it seemed as if my

surfboard, legs, and feet were all connected as one body.

As I dropped in to these smooth walled up waves, the power was balanced perfectly from the bottom turn to the hard carving high speed top turns. This was free riding, soul surfing bliss. It was like drawing a fluid smooth analog line down the wave face and finding power pockets to fit the rocker of the board. The surfboard and I became an arc of fusion and explosion onto the invisible force that's making the water stand up as a wave. This was the ultimate day. But little did I know I was about to get the ultimate wave I ever surfed.

The wave was turquoise green, walled up to eight feet in height, and seemed as though it was too big for the sand bar. I was in the right spot at the right time. Digging in deep to paddle hard with my arms, the board began to slide down the green face. The wave stood up fast and as I pushed up and planted my feet to the waxy top of my board which took all of my focus and senses to feel what line to draw on this one. As soon as I was standing, the glassy water in front of the wave seemed to flow off of the sandbar and feed the belly of this beast.

With the suddenness of a thunderstorm the curtain of shimmering water turned gold from the low Sun then it surrounded me and just like that I was locked in. The view from inside the tube was like a huge tear drop opening moving in a fluid stream of clear gold, blue, and emerald green sparkling in the winter sun. The sound inside of this green room was like the close roar of thunder, almost like a trumpet combined with buckets of water poured out into a pool.

After a long time inside of this bubble of moving water, better known as a tube ride, the opening got larger and I was spit out. The feeling was brilliant! Pure stoke of joy ran through my veins at that moment. But this soul surfing experience was just getting started. The wave threw a bright golden curtain over me again, and once again time itself seemed to stand still.

The intensity of this tube ride was becoming magnified in the survival instinct of my entire being. The wave seemed to double in power and thickness, and now the bright colors became dark. The sunlight seemed to disappear and the dirtiness of a tornado filled the barrel as it seemed to growl at me with explosions of brown sand blown water.

After what seemed like ions of time the blurred opening became clearer and clearer when suddenly a blast of mist and foam flew past me and the escape from this cave of darkness was done. The feeling at this point was pureness of stoke like laughing so hard that you tear up.

This was already the best ride I ever had so far, but it wouldn't stop. It just kept forming up and recreating itself over and over into new perfection. After a natural curve of drawing out some smooth powerhouse knife edge turns, on this smooth canvas, sheets of salty water flew high up into the air, then the wave took over again and consumed me into its belly.

This third stand-up tube ride was a smooth, clean, deep green fluid motion of perfection. This time I dragged my hand on the ceiling of this glassy tube as it was like standing behind a waterfall, it just kept spinning and standing up in the shape of a green glass cave. After a long drawn out ride inside of this one I escaped again but then it looked like it was going to close out ahead me.

Completely satisfied by what this wave gave me, I was now willing to sacrifice myself and prepared for some serious beatings because it appeared the wave was going to break one hundred feet all at once. Just going for it I built up every ounce of speed I had as the wave threw a thick wall of salty dark green water over and around me. This was the deepest I had ever been I the tube!

The wave jacked up even bigger than the start and now it was a roaring monster and it was sand blasting the freshly built sandbar. Feeling like this was the end of this amazing journey I was ready to give up but a deep intuition was telling me to stay on my board.

After rings of barreling torrents encircled me, whitewater engulfed and swallowed me up. Vision was lost and breathing was stopped as the preparation for judgment seemed sure. But something bright filled my blurred sight, as now the vision of escape once again seemed possible. I was outrunning the consuming whitewater ball inside of the tube and was now inside of the most amazing tunnel of moving liquid glass imaginable. This tube ride was the longer of the others as it seemed like minutes of looking at this room of fluid motion which was changing from silvery gem to sparkling sun spots as the escape happened.

Knowing that the beach was getting close, I could see the guys out at the hook looking over at me, and I heard them yelling out a cheer.

It was time for another sweet tube ride. This time it was a little thinner, but an awesome barrel. The glassy tear drop opening spun to an end and the wave was ready to close out. After being shot out of that last tube, it seemed as though I was flying and so I drew a long bottom turn and projected up to the collapsing lip and carved a hard arching full-rail-turn under the final close out curtain of sea water. Then I disappeared into the white foaming turbulence. Everything was a grey blur with my eyes open, the sound was still, then I realized I had made it, I pulled off the most radical turn on the most amazing wave I had ever rode.

"That was the ultimate experience in my life", I thought. That day I had finally found what I was searching for. This was the wave that brought complete peace and happiness to my soul at that moment.

Now we will travel back to the day I was born.

My mother gave birth to me at the old county hospital, on Emmeline street in Santa Cruz, July of 1970.

Santa Cruz was paradise in those days. Imagine a place with a Mediterranean climate, laid back culture, and uncrowded beaches. Now combine that with the most beautiful misty redwood forested mountains, flowing with emerald green streams, pristine beaches, perfect point breaks for surfing, health food stores, and places like the Cooper House with fresh live music.

Anyone who was there remembers it well. The general vibe was so laid back. All seemed so wonderful but at the same time drugs were becoming a problem. Many young people were experimenting with drugs.

They were searching for deeper meaning to life looking into the spiritual side of life. They tried many different kinds of drugs to find spiritual answers to life.

What's life all about?

There must be a purpose, right?

Where did we come from?

Where are we going?

Many found out the drugs opened their minds to many philosophies and even made them feel satisfied for a time but all these ways seemed to lead to a dead end. Many overdosed on drugs and died.

My parents were there and they were in the deep end of this culture. They were there at the Santa Cruz and San Francisco Fillmore rock concerts. They surfed, hung out with the other locals smoking dope and searching for perfect waves.

They took illegal drugs, including Heroin, LSD, Cocaine, anything they could "Score". My mom found herself addicted to heroin and overdosed one time in a cave at Big Sur. So my parents started to find themselves trapped in this dark gloomy world of drugs.

My mom ran away from home when she was a very young teen. She and her sister had a stepfather from Greece who was chasing them and trying to molest them. So she ran away from home to be free from this monster. She ran away from it all.

She was young but street smart. She was able to get a job and support herself through her teenage years. She ended up like many in her generation taking drugs.

My dad and her met and fell in love in 1969. My dad was a soul surfer and a hippie drop out. My mother became pregnant and was still addicted to drugs.

They ended up realizing they had dead end lives and needed help. They found help, healing and new life.

During this time in Santa Cruz a new organization was getting started to help young people escape their drug problems. It was started and led by a talented African American man named Gene Dawson. The name of the program was the DAPC, "Drug Abuse Prevention Center."

Gene was a gifted man who helped young people stop their self-destruction in Drugs.

Much like Chuck Smith at Calvary Chapel in southern

California was used by God to help young hippies find a new life in Jesus, so too was Gene.

During this time Gene prayed for my mother and father and through the power of Jesus they were freed and healed from the chains of drugs. It was one step, as they were "Born Again" into new life by the Spirit of God. The grip the hard drugs had on their souls was peeled away and released by the Spirit of God.

While my mother was pregnant with me she prayed, "Lord if you keep my baby from the harm of all those drugs then I will dedicate him to you".

They never took drugs again and this was a great miracle. There were other great miracles like this happening in their generation. This period of time was marked by many as the "Jesus Movement". What a great name for it. It was a revival. The revival was a generation revived by Jesus from spiritual darkness.

This doesn't mean that they were seeking God so much that he was revived because God never sleeps or slumbers. The Bible makes that very clear.

So how did this revival happen and what did it look like?

First of all, the people were revived, not God. He is the

same yesterday, today, and forever. We humans are the ones who sleep and slumber. We are blind to God as we focus in on ourselves, our achievements, our world, our community, other gods, religion, materialism, politics, the environment, animals and humans.

Up and down the West Coast during this time a Jesus revival was flourishing. Young people were seeking truth about the meaning of life and many were finding it.

They were certainly not finding it in drugs. They were not finding it in the religions of the world. They were not finding it in the colleges. Not in the American dream. Not in the Liberal dream. Not in communism. No, they were only finding it in Jesus.

During those early years in the 1970's, I remember as a little child sensing the very presence of God's Spirit.

One night especially I experienced God's powerful, yet peaceful presence.

We lived and worked in the old Twin Lakes Church buildings just up the street from Twin Lakes Beach. On Friday nights we had worship in the Garden room. There were about four hundred people there singing and worshiping God to the sweet sounding instruments of our gifted worship leaders.

While the parents and other young hippies were praising God, we little children were in the gymnasium next to the Garden room.

I must have been four or five years old and experienced the holy presence of God. There was this heavy yet wonderful peace in the air. The gym was dark except for the warm light of the Garden room spilling out into the darkened gym. We played in that gym for about an hour then it was nap time. The teachers laid out some mats on the floor for us to sleep. As I walked over to where the mats were I felt the goodness, the sweetness of God in that place.

There was a warmness and peace in my chest and I knew at that tender age that it was God. The Holy Spirit was dwelling there that night in an awesome way. As I laid down to go to sleep, my joy filled eyes looked up above the double doors of the gym and I could see a glowing blue clear presence like misty clouds moving around up near the ceiling.

In the middle of the worship music I drifted to sleep seeing these angelic beings joyfully flying around to the praises of God. They seemed to fly like doves in the early morning light as they flutter their bright wings. It was just for a moment but I saw what I saw and it was good.

That same year a couple of strangers came to our Twin Lakes center. These two peculiar men had a sweet peace about them. They just had a joy and love from God that everyone was drawn to. The little children surrounded these two joy filled men and the men made each one of them smile. They told many stories about how good God is and the children sat around them listening intently.

During that afternoon I was by myself roaming the halls looking for other kids to play with. I heard the two of them in the gym telling the stories to the large group of children gathered around them.

My dad was the Director of this building at that time and he invited them to stay for dinner. As all of the children gathered around them listening to one of them talk about God, I peeked around the double doors to see what was going on. Earlier I had sensed that there was something special, something powerful about these two. I had seen many different strangers come off of the street but these two were different.

As I peeked around the corner of the double doors the man telling the story immediately stopped, turned his head toward me and smiled.

He said, "Don't be afraid. Come here little one, and join

us".

I knew as a little child he was good and kind. I knew he had the power of God inside of him. So I joined in the crowd of children as he told us stories. He kept looking at me with a gleaming sunshine filled smile as he told them stories.

Later that night my mom prepared a special meal for the guests and all of the residents. Steak was donated to our not-for-profit ministry and my mom was by far the best cook in our ministry organization.

I remember the two men sat at our table for this community dinner. My dad and mom were sitting there along with some of the other staff members enjoying this great meal together.

Suddenly I began to choke on a piece of steak. This was a bad situation because it was lodged deep in the wind pipe. I stayed still and no one noticed that I was choking for a long time.

Later on in life my mother told me that I was all blue by the time she was aware I was choking.

By the time everyone noticed I was choking it had been well over a minute. Everyone seemed to be in shock and not knowing what to do. These were the days when people didn't have the First Aid training like they do today so everybody just looked at me with ghostly white faces. This was well before the Heimlich Maneuver was made popular.

The choking continued when suddenly one of the strangers calmly yet swiftly got up and walked over to me. He picked me up and grabbed me by my ankles and moved me up and down about a foot's distance off of the floor. It only took a few shakes and the piece of steak dislodged and fell out of my mouth.

The man then flipped me back over hugged me and handed over to my mother. My mom and dad were so thankful for what just happened. Of all nights to be there, this stranger who knew what to do was there at our table to save my life.

Shortly after that the two men left and we never saw them again.

Who were these men?

I don't know but I believe God had sent them that day to help.

A few months after the choking incident there was another display of God's great grace in my life.

One sunny late morning I was walking along down the south end of the Twin Lakes building hallway just having a great day. Out of nowhere a large strong man grabbed me by the throat. His large hand clamped around my neck like a vice.

Here I was a helpless little five-year-old boy being hoisted up in the air by this violent evil eyed killer.

I remember looking into his eyes and all I saw was darkness, a deep oily darkness of evil seemed to exude out of his two portals.

As his strong tattooed hand squeezed tighter and tighter, I remember thinking I was about to die. The pressure he put on my neck felt like he was going to snap it.

From my view I was so high up in the air that it seemed like I was going to hit the ceiling of the hallway. I could see his evil smile that turned to laughter as he was no doubt about to murder me.

As he was enjoying his malicious moment watching me suffocate he suddenly turned his head to the left. His gaze turned from laughing-evil to scared-to-death. He seemed to turn from looking at me to someone else much bigger and tougher than him.

His face turned milky white, as he screamed in fear. Immediately his heinous death grip on me released and I free fell down toward the hard floor. I remember landing as if on giant soft pillows.

The man screamed and trembled in consuming fear. He turned and ran down the hall screaming toward the south exit. I felt no fear, no pain, and was glad he was gone. I looked to see who scared him and no one was there.

I got up just like any little boy would and joyfully walked back down the hall looking for my buddies to play with.

Was this God's gracious protecting hand again?

My guess is one big, yes.

A few years later my little brother and I got to stay with our grandpa Harvey for a few days.

Grandpa Harvey was a U.S Army World War Two, Korea, and Vietnam war veteran who retired as a Master Sergeant.

He was the best. He had a way of making you feel good and at ease just being near him. He loved my brother and I deeply and loved to show us off at the local Veterans Hall.

Every time we stayed with him he would take us straight to the garage for military standard haircuts. My parents were typical surfer hippie types and so we always showed up with long sun bleached blonde hair. Grandpa would immediately escort us into his makeshift barber shop and "Buzz" – military standard haircuts completed.

He always took us to his local church. I remember he was a volunteer handyman for the church as he was constantly fixing things there.

He loved to sing thunderously during the worship time. It wasn't a boastful singing but more of a proclaiming of "I am not ashamed to sing to Jesus".

I remember one song in particular as it still rings clearly in my ears because of the way he sang it. It was, "Onward Christian soldiers, marching as to war, with the Cross of Jesus going on before…"

He thundered it out like a bold lion, yet with the friendliest smile in the whole church.

I loved my grandpa dearly. I loved how he loved people. He just overflowed with love and joy like a fountain.

I remember how he hugged us with a big smile. I loved his mustache that reached from cheek to cheek with sharp point on the ends. I loved how he tended his garden of strawberries, and his vineyard of wine grapes in the backyard.

My brother and I got to stay for a three-day visit and he asked us what we wanted to do. We told him right away that we wanted to go to Marriot's Great America.

This was the central California's biggest and best theme park. Every time we drove past it on the freeway my brother and I were mesmerized by the giant rollercoasters.

Grandpa smiled big and said "Alright boys, let's go".

Grandma wasn't so happy about that. She was worried about his heart because he had numerous heart attacks in the past few years. But grandpa insisted, "Great America it is boys".

The next day we spent all day at the amusement park. He was having so much fun. He went on all of the fast roller coasters that a nine-year-old was allowed to go on.

We watched one of the earliest giant movie screens which was a big deal in 1979. We ate hamburgers and ice cream; we played the arcade games and shooting games; and rode the bumper cars. It was truly great.

My grandpa was so happy that day. He was so filled with enthusiasm and joy because he loved my brother and I the only way a grandpa could.

After dinner and baths we were all ready for a good night's sleep. Grandma tucked my tired brother and I into our beds. Then grandpa came in to read us a story and pray with us. We faded and sank into the sweetest sleep.

I remember reflecting on how it was a day that every little boy dreams of having. It was one of the best days of my life. Ah, off to sleep I went.

Waking up slow and easy I was overwhelmed with good feelings deep in my heart. This warm peaceful felling in my heart and soul were of God's peace. I could literally see the peace and joy in my room that sparkled and shined right into my heart.

It was the middle of the night. My room was dark yet a blueish warm glow of sparkling light filled the whole room. It was that same warm love of God's presence I felt in that gym years earlier at the Twin Lakes Center.

I knew that an angel from Heaven was standing right there at the foot of our beds watching over us.

I climbed out of bed with no fear and just felt at ease next to this gentle giant being from heaven. As I walked toward the door I felt his hand on my shoulder.

Then I remember we were looking down the hall and I could hear men's voices yelling out, "Stay with us Harvey, you need to stay with us. Harvey, can you hear me?"

Then I heard, "One and, two and, three and, four and." I also heard my grandmother crying out, "No Harvey, no Harvey". The stretcher rolled past us and the firemen and paramedics were giving my grandpa CPR.

Remembering back on that moment and none of them noticed me standing there. Seeing all of this brought no fear or sadness in me because the overwhelming love and peace of God was in my heart.

I remember turning around and moving back toward my bed with utter joy and rest in my soul. I remember settling into my bed with a smile on my face as this time an angel from God was tucking me into bed. This was the sweetest most restful sleep I have ever had. I was smiling with an ocean of joy and peace as I settled into a deep sleep.

The next morning my brother and I woke up and headed out into the living room. There we saw my mom and dad sitting on the couch with my sobbing grandma. My mom was holding her and my dad came over to us and said, "Grandpa died last night."

Two weeks later was his funeral service. As we drove into the cemetery the sun was shining and clusters of pigeons fluttered their wings as they flew up into the sky. There was a group of soldiers in their formal uniforms with rifles over their shoulders.

My dad hastily parked the pickup truck. My mom got out followed by my dad. He asked my brother and I if we wanted to go or stay in the truck. We stayed there and had a view of the ceremony. As they played "Taps", my brother began to bawl. He wept loudly as the tears rand down his face like rain on the windshield. I understood that it was good to cry and I knew he needed to.

He looked over at me and said angrily, "Didn't you love grandpa? Why aren't you crying?

I told him about the angel the night he died and how good it was. I told him about how peaceful and sweet it was. I tried to explain that I wished I was there with him because it was so good. I was sad too, but the fresh memory of that night overwhelmed me.

He didn't understand and I stopped talking about it and never told anyone else about this until recently.

The Same Today

Chapter Two: Seeds to New Life

Winds of change were in the air. My dad was talking about New Mexico often. He was listening to country music and seemed to be drawn to the South West as if it were still the old west.

It was 1979 and we were preparing to move to Albuquerque, New Mexico to start a ministry through our Santa Cruz church. So, just like that, we were on our way to Albuquerque.

I always liked the whole cowboy thing as a little boy. And so that was the vision I had of this southwest city.

It was strange seeing endless miles of brown desert because Santa Cruz was lush and green all the year round.

We drove through much of the old Route 66 which was replaced by the larger Interstate 40. We started to see classic high desert scenes such as, buttes and mesas. The rocks started to paint red hues like the inside of watermelon.

We started to see adobe-styled homes as we neared Gallup, New Mexico. We drove through part of the old route 66 to a motel in Gallup. This cowboy town had the classic neon lights glowing down the main street with the red painted desert as a backdrop. We were starting to feel the whole Southwest culture.

Then we arrived in Albuquerque and it was the largest city since leaving Santa Cruz. We drove over the Rio Grande River and off to our right we could see a couple of high rise buildings glimmering in the afternoon sunlight. Straight ahead to the east we saw the watermelon red sun-painted Sandia Mountains.

We drew closer to the mountains which had a dusting of crisp bright white snow on top. We turned off of the interstate highway and headed north on a road called Eubank. Then onto Conches Avenue where we saw our home-to-be for the next four years. It was a classic desert brown adobe-style house of about fifteen years old.

We had a lot of fun as a family in New Mexico. We fished the Conches Lake, Elephant Butte Lake, and the little Pecos River for trout. We hiked the trails in the foothills of the mountains. We rode on the Tramway up to the summit of the Sandia Mountains. We played in the snow. It was all such a great adventure exploring new places together.

Some of best memories were mule-deer hunting with my dad. We hunted the desert mountains and saw scenes right out of the famous Old West paintings.

One day we reached the summit of the Jicarilla Mountain range and one side was covered in snow. The sun was getting low so the snow was highlighted by the gold and flaming red hues when suddenly a large heard of mule deer ran down the mountain in the snow. They gracefully descended down the turquoise hue of the snowy shadow of the mountain like a cascading waterfall. A large racked Buck was in the lead of this cascading herd. We just watched in awe of this classic, timeless southwest scene.

So we fully experienced the great southwest State of New Mexico to the fullest and we loved it.

A few of years later I was watching a Sunkist orange soda commercial on T.V. and I saw surfers riding the turquoise sun sparkling waves. I saw the warm white sandy beaches again. This triggered something in my soul and I wanted to be there again and go surfing. So I started to skateboard all over town pretending I was surfing the waves.

My friends quickly bought skateboards after me and we tore up the town. Albuquerque was a skateboarder's paradise in those days. The whole town had these perfectly rounded concrete finished drain ditches. They were clean from the routine flashfloods that swept through them. They were all a little different and had the same feel as riding an eight-foot wave at the famous surf spot called, "Steamer Lane" in Santa Cruz. In my mind I was surfing Steamer Lane while carving on the smooth concrete walls of Albuquerque. The occasional tumble weed would roll by reminding me I was far from the beaches of Santa Cruz.

Albuquerque was one big skateboard park in those days. It was open to the public and no one cared if you wanted to skateboard through it.

This desire for surfing was growing in my soul.

That summer we visited our former home of Santa Cruz. I remember as we drove into town the rich salty ocean air mixed with the smell of the sandy beach. This filled my soul with bliss.

On our visit, my dad rented a surfboard from an old gas

station near Cowells Beach. We surfed the river mouth where I learned to stand up and ride the waves for the first time.

I hated going back to New Mexico, but back we went and I told my friends all about the surfing in Santa Cruz. They were all really interested and wanted to go with me on our next trip.

Around this time, I was around twelve years old and felt like I was becoming an independent man. I also began to rebel against my parents and got into trouble.

I stole my dad's M80's fireworks so my friends and I blew up mail boxes, real estate signs, and just about anything else we felt like destroying.

One day we started a fire in my friend's apartment complex dumpster and watched the fire department come to put it out. We would walk around at night and throw baseball size rocks at peoples living room windows.

Another day I stole a coffee can full of my dad's black powder for his muzzle loader riffle. My friends and I were going to make a super-sized M80 and blow up the back wall of the supermarket. We stuffed a bunch of moist tissues in the can around the M80 on the top, above the packed gunpowder.

As my friends watched me from the other side of the concrete wall I lit the bomb and ran like "hell" over to them. We all watched as it went boom and a large white mushroom cloud ascended high like a mini nuclear bomb.

To our disappointment it just put big black mark on the cinder-block wall.

On another day my friends and I were thinking of how we could cause more trouble in the town. We were at my friend Anthony's house and he told us about this really scary game that his parents had. He said it was stored away in their attic and it really freaked him out.

It was called an Ouija Board, also known as a "Spirit Board" or "Talking Board".

We began to pressure him into getting that game out of the attic, but he was so scared he began to cry. Then our curiosity grew all the more because of his fear.

He finally gave in and took it out of box in the attic. We took it from him and headed over to my friend's house who lived in the low income apartments. He said his mom had experience in that kind of stuff.

Something in me began to tell me this was wrong but I didn't bother listening to that.

So we took it to his apartment and his mother sat in her

chair encouraging us to do this. She even recommended we get one of the old antique blankets off of her bed and spread it out on the floor. She then closed the curtains, turned off the lights and gave us candles to light while we played that weird game.

She knew all about this Ouija game and showed us how to play it in the dark, candle lit room. Immediately the air felt cold in the darkness of that room. Some of the kids were freaked out. I was more curious than scared and so we continued.

As soon as we began to play, a woman screamed at the top of her lungs from the downstairs apartment. My friend's mother sat in her chair and said, "You see, there is power in it." At that point, it got too weird for me. I wasn't scared but I didn't like what was happening. So I pulled up the blanket and said that's enough.

I never did anything with that kid again. I had a new group of friends who were into fighting and girls more than anything else. In fact, when I saw that kid again, right or wrong, I wanted to fight him. I remember chasing him across the Conches Park, to his apartment.

My friend Anthony had good sense about him as he hated the evil that the Ouija board could fester up. His parents believed in Jesus and so did he.

I was living outside of a relationship with God and deep down I knew it.

I started to get into fighting and drinking beer, and hard liquor. I was quickly heading down the wrong road at the age of twelve.

It was 1982 and my dad was away a lot because of the business he was in. He made long road trips up into Iowa and Pennsylvania to purchase antiques for resale. He was good at it but it took a lot of his time.

So my mom knew we needed a good Jesus-centered Bible teaching church and she found one. It was a very small church in a small space. It was as if they put up some chairs in an old liquor store at a small strip mall. It immediately reminded me of our church in Santa Cruz.

I remember our first visit. I looked around and saw that the worship style and general feel was just like the days in the early 70's. I thought, "Oh great, look at all these Jesus freaks with their hands up in the air like antennas.

I hated it because my heart was hard toward Jesus. I sat there with my arms crossed just bored out of my mind. I was determined to shut it all out.

But when the teacher got up and read from the Bible

something was happening. He was a tall, skinny blonde haired surfer looking dude with a big smile named, Skip Heitzig. He looked like he could have been one of the local boys from Santa Cruz.

When he taught through the Bible, the words seemed like seeds on my heart. Even though I resisted the words they stuck with me. I remember I hated him. I didn't know why but I could not stand this guy.

After one of the services my mom was talking to Skip and he looked at me with a friendly smile and said, "Hey, how are you?"

I just looked at him and brushed him off in my mind even though I knew he was a man full of the love of God.

Sitting in that place, time after time, listening to Skip teach the word of God didn't seem to be doing anything for me. In my mind I wasn't going have any of that Jesus stuff.

My dad came home from one of his long trips with a truck and trailer full of antiques. He would work on restoring much of the furniture out in our back yard. He was an excellent craftsman in wood work and restoration. So as he refinished the antiques while at the same time he listened to tapes of Chuck Smith teaching through the Bible from Calvary Chapel, in California.

So I started getting a double dose of this word of God. I couldn't escape it. It was as if Jesus was pursuing me. Though I started out resisting the teachings, I do remember I started to soften my heart and began to distance myself from my rowdy friends.

Shortly after this time my dad and mom announced to my brother and I that we were moving to Tucson, Arizona. We were going to "Plant" another ministry center with some friends from our home church of Santa Cruz.

The leader of our "Drug Abuse and Preventive Center" had changed the name of it to "Grapevine Ministries".

We were to start this new ministry outreach supported by donations and a local thrift store. So we welcomed a new family from Santa Cruz, to take over our location in Albuquerque. We packed up and headed for Tucson.

The partner family happened to be our old friends from Santa Cruz, so my parents were excited about this opportunity. I really didn't care about the ministry. I just wanted to move back to Santa Cruz so I could surf.

So we arrived in Tucson and I was surprised by how much it looked like southern California. It reminded me of Ventura with all of the Palm trees and bright sun.

The family was with us in the early 70's during the

whole Jesus movement. They were an awesome Italian family. The Mom of that family was my first grade teacher and was more like an aunt to me.

When we arrived they were very happy to see us.

They already had the house rented and were living in half of it. It was an old two story house that used to be a frat house for the University of Arizona which was just a few blocks down the street. It was a classic old house with hard wood floors and lots of windows. But it had no air conditioning and lots of cockroaches.

The day we arrived I grabbed my skateboard and headed for the University campus which was only a five-minute skateboard ride away. Near the entrance of the campus I found a Surf and Skateboard shop. I was so stoked about this.

I enjoyed the University because it had a good feel about it. I just felt like I was one of the students even though I was thirteen. I was hanging around the pool and got to know the college students who worked there. I would even run the pool register while they had to go study or just wanted a break.

Back at the ministry house I was a very disrespectful and unruly kid. I didn't care about much of anything but what I wanted to do. But at the same time there was something different going on inside of me. I felt like I needed God. I needed to have a relationship with Jesus Christ.

One day the whole house got together for a Bible study and prayer time. Afterward my dad and his partner Jim were both in the kitchen of that old home talking. My brother and I walked in and the two of them were looking at us intently. Then Jim said, "You need to get saved, you really need to be 'born again'".

It pierced my heart when he said that because I knew it was true. I was struggling with that in my mind for the past few months because of all the teaching from the Bible by Skip. I just needed someone to be bold enough to say it like he just did.

It was not Jim who was saying it into my heart but the Holy Spirit of God. I knew it was God speaking through him. I knew it had nothing to do with Jim or any man but it was business between me and God. It was real.

I felt this gentle touch, this knock on the door of my heart that I can say was God. He was putting the spotlight from heaven right on my heart and I knew it.

So I walked over to my dad and Jim and said, "Yes its

true I need to be saved and I want to be saved".

So they put their hands on my shoulder and led me to pray a simple prayer to surrender my life to Jesus and become "Born Again".

As they prayed for me I began to feel this heavy weight being lifted off of me.

Imagine it like this: It was like this giant dirty bag that weighed ten tons and contained all of my sins which looked like a tangled string of black oily, smelly, repulsive waste was all at once lifted off of my shoulders and catapulted light years into outer space.

All of my sin was gone. I was free like never before.

I felt fresh and clean like a new born baby. It was as if it was the dawn of a gorgeous new day. Like a clear sunny morning after a rain. It was like being under muddy water and emerging out into the clear, fresh warm air to breath.

After I said those words out loud and from my heart, simply asking Jesus to forgive me, calling him my Lord and Savior I experienced a deep peace and satisfaction in my spirit.

I felt so much peace that hour. It was as if God had opened the door to heaven and shined his Son's light into my soul. It was like a candle being lit and becoming warm from the core as it softens from the inside out. Then the fragrant sweet aroma from the burning candle rises to the Heavens.

I know that this experience is not the same for everyone nor should it be. Some feel nothing when they pray this prayer but they have legitimately been born again. The common ingredient is His love. The beginning of a lifelong loving relationship with Jesus. This is evident by some good fruit in their lives because there is a change from the old ways of my heart to the new life of following Jesus Christ.

After I prayed the prayer of salvation, they prayed for the Holy Spirit to fill me up.

I stood there in the light of God's presence as his warm presence shined and poured into my spirit. It was His great love that I experienced in my heart. The Holy Spirit just filled my heart like fire. It was like a fire was lit and began to burn in my heart in this good way, it was God's pure glorious grace.

Imagine it like the warm waves of the Caribbean Sea washing over you, so was this experience, this filling of the Holy Spirit. I was in a perfect state of utter peace, happiness, and goodness.

After I was done praying my brother walked over to them and gave his life to the Lord. As they began to pray for him, I was filled with so much joy that I had to leave the room.

So I went to the main bathroom of that old house, shut and locked the door. I fell to my knees and lifted my hands up to the Lord and began thanking him over and over with tears of joy streaming down my face.

Immediately I had a new attitude. I was respectful to my dad and mom. I was enjoying being a young man for the first time. Instead of fighting, blowing up mail boxes, or playing with satanic games like the Ouija board, I was reading the Bible and enjoying it. I was reading God's word, praying often, and listening to and obeying my parents.

The next day I helped my dad with our ministry business. Furniture was often donated for our thrift store we ran which was located at the Old downtown Tucson area.

As my dad and I rode around together that day I remember asking him about the Jewish people and Israel. I had just read in my Bible how they were God's people. I found that I had this natural love for them that came from God. It was His love planted in my heart that showed me this. So I knew that it was from God: to love His people.

You too can open the door of your heart to Jesus by saying this simple prayer from your heart: "Lord I am a sinner. Please forgive me. I give you my life. I believe in Jesus Christ as my Lord and savior. I believe He died on the cross and shed His blood for me. I believe He rose from the grave. I believe He is alive right now. I choose to follow you in Jesus name. Amen."

Chapter Three: Surfing the World

By 1984 my dad and Jim began to disagree on many things. There seemed to be this growing chasm between them and everyone in the house knew it.

Jim was beginning to act strange. He was trying to control everyone in the ministry house. He wanted total submission to him as if that was the same as total submission to Christ.

Thank God my dad wasn't going for it. Jim's type of leadership was misguided and blind much like the Pharisees during Jesus time on earth. So my father called him out on his crazy thinking. This ended up painting my dad in a bad light because Jim was one of the ministry leader's favorites.

One horrible, tension filled night was the peak of this

mountainous wave of disagreement. Both families were at our downtown thrift store and Jim wanted to have a meeting with my dad and little brother. I was sitting in a couch up near the front of the store while I heard the arguing grow louder and louder.

Then Jim just seemed to lose his mind and yelled out at my dad, "You need to break".

My dad was cool-headed and just looked at Jim while he acted like a spoiled little boy who couldn't get his way.

Then Jim really lost it. He stepped up his bullying tactics and yelled at the top of his lungs, "You either break or I will have you and your family out on the streets".

Jim was basically saying, "Submit to my authority or I will make your family homeless".

My father kept his cool but was blown away that his friend who was used by God, had now turned into this tyrant. I think it broke my dad's heart but it never broke his relationship with Jesus Christ. My dad knew that God was with our family and he did not allow this crazed man to hurt our family.

So my dad and mom quickly moved us out of that place and we headed back to our hometown of Santa Cruz, California.

I love and respect my dad for putting his family before the ministry.

Many in this ministry we called the "Center" seemed to believe that ministry was the same thing as God himself. They basically started to believe that ministry was God.

So if you cut ties with the ministry you were thought of as cutting ties with God.

How wrong is that?

God is not ministry. Your service or works is never the same as your salvation. You can never earn it because you can only be saved by the free gift of grace that comes through believing in Jesus Christ as your Lord and Savior.

In the Bible, John and Paul wrote much about this. In John's gospel the word "Believe" is penned ninety-nine times. By faith believing in Jesus is what makes you righteous. This was made very clear by Paul in the book of Romans chapter four:

For if Abraham was justified by works, he has something to boast about, but not before God. For what does the scripture say? "For Abraham believed God and it was credited to him as righteousness." Now to the one who works, his wage is not credited as a favor, but as what is due. But to the one who does not work, but believes in Him who justifies the ungodly, his faith is credited as righteousness.

So God is God and your saving relationship with him is not dependent on how much you work for him.

Anyone who teaches otherwise is in great error. They are directly defying God's good grace. Otherwise we make what Jesus did on the cross meaningless. He paid and paved our way into paradise by the shedding of his own blood. It was by his sweat not by yours that the great work of restoring you to God was accomplished. Remember in the Garden just before going to the cross he sweat blood while his closest followers slept.

Then at the end of his great work on the cross he said, "It is finished." At that very moment the great veil of the temple was torn from top to bottom and free access to God was through the work Jesus did.

He didn't say, "You must do", he said, "It is finished."

Yes, James wrote in the New Testament, "Faith without works is dead". Yet it's how you define "Works" that makes it relevant.

Jesus said, "Come to Me, all you who labor and are heavy

laden, and I will give you rest. Take My yoke upon you and learn from Me, for I am gentle and lowly in heart, and you will find rest for your souls. For My yoke is easy and My burden is light."

Did you see that?

He said, "My Yoke is easy and My burden is light." The Yoke was the piece of wood that was on the shoulders of the Oxen used for pulling the plow. It's like the cross. Remember Jesus carried the wood on His shoulders as he worked hard to carry it to His death. Our sins were upon His shoulders. He did all of the heavy lifting so we could be forgiven and set free.

He also said that Mary, who was sitting with him was doing the better thing than her sister Martha who was sweating in the kitchen trying to prepare a meal.

How hard was Mary working?

She wasn't working at all but just being with and listening to Him. That was her work of faith. She was taking his yoke which was easy and light. She was finding rest while her sister was struggling to serve the Lord.

Everyone is unique. You have a fingerprint unique to you. Your personality is also one of a kind and not exactly like any other. In that same way, your work is unique to the Lord. So your works will never look exactly like others.

This is the problem with many Christians especially in

ministry. Many ministry leaders who go bad think they need followers who look just like them.

The only thing that must be the same in all followers of Christ, is God's love. God is love, and He is full of loving kindness and tender mercies. Love is His very nature and if He lives in our spirit then that love will blossom into His good sweet fruit.

God's love planted in our hearts is the fruit of the Spirit. It all stems from Him, His Spirit, that third person of the Trinity, the Holy Spirit. He fills our dead, deflated sails which is a picture of our dead spirits being brought to life by God's breath, His wind beneath our wings, His sweet Holy Spirit. So we who are saved were the dead branches, but then we were grafted in to Him and we became alive as we blossomed from Him.

As our sail or spirit is filled by His wind or Spirit of God and He pushes us gently forward pointing us toward Jesus. We are locked on course and anchored to Jesus. Jesus is that solid rock that we are anchored to. So our anchor line is our branch, so to speak, now grafted into Him.

So the whole point of this is that Jesus is kind and forgiving. He's not standing around waiting for you to mess up so he can judge you. Isaiah prophesied about him, "A bruised reed He would not break".

Are you a "Bruised" person? Have you had your heart broken?

I have too, but there is hope.

He made a way for you to live forever in paradise.

How do you and I get there?

It's easier than you think because Jesus said, "I am the Way, the Truth and the life, no one comes to the Father except by Me". He also said, "My yoke is easy and light". God just requires that you believe in him as your Lord and Savior. The religious leaders were making the "Yoke" hard and heavy. They were being harsh by breaking the bruised reeds which were the struggling common people like you and me.

The ministry that started out so good had turned bad. The elders of "Grapevine" or the "Center" had become Pharisees. So God humbled many of them for becoming so arrogant.

So here we were back in Santa Cruz. It was so good to be home. Ah yes, the smell of the ocean air, the mystic redwoods, the old beach houses, the surf roaring at night, the sound of the fog horn at the harbor, yes this was home.

We lived on Branciforte Drive which was midtown Santa Cruz.

My best friend Sam, from among the Center kids started surfing with me. We surfed all over town whenever we could but our closest spot was the San Lorenzo River mouth. So, we surfed there most of the time.

I remember a rainy day in the middle of January the river was chocolate brown with entire redwood trees floating down it at a fast rate. So my friend Sam and I jumped in the raging river from Pearl street near his house and we were rushed out to sea within minutes. We surfed these stormy waves while trying to avoid stumps, trees, and branches and we had a great time.

I started attending Harbor High School which was the midtown locals' school. I remember we had some of the best surfers in town such as, Josh Mulcoy, Josh Loya, Shane Desmond and a bunch more.

As a family we were still connected to the "Grapevine" ministry we called the "Center". We took over a group home which was loosely connected to that ministry. This helped us become more independent.

This group home was tough. It was made up of troubled teenage boys. Imagine living with a bunch of teenage boys and many of them from the criminal justice system. This was our home environment. It was tough but it was good for my brother and I. We were "Street smart", because of this experience.

Surfing became everything to me. It was the way to happiness as far as I was concerned. I started to get pretty good at it by my junior year in high school. I became immersed in this surf culture.

I distanced myself from the Center teens I had grown up with, and met a new friend, named Seth. He and I would surf every day. His step dad was an excellent surfer and well known surfboard shaper and so he made all of our boards custom for us. We were both sponsored by his dad who shaped "Taylor Made Surfboards". We also were sponsored by Santa Cruz Surf Shop and Rip Curl wetsuits.

My friend Seth was a great guy and a powerful surfer. I really enjoyed the years of hanging out with him and his parents. His mom was a sweet lady who took us down to southern California to compete in the surf contests to places like Oceanside.

We were a tight knit surfing community in those days. The surfers all knew each other across town and when we ventured down to southern California for surf contests we stuck together as one band of brothers representing Santa Cruz. Sure, we were the Westside, Midtown, and Eastside locals, but when we left town we were the Santa Cruz locals.

My friend, "Skin dog" or "Skinny" as we called him was best friends with Jeff Lansing, and the two of them made up the best comedy show you could imagine.

I remember a trip we took down to Malibu for a surf contest one summer with Skin Dog, Jeff Lansing, Joran, and myself. These guys were ballsy, tough, and one of a kind. What I loved about these guys was how they were their own unique person and they could care less if anyone like them or not. They had their own unique style on the waves, and on land.

The sweet thing is we all have our own unique style in life. Ever wonder why fingerprints are used for identity? It is because they are completely unique to you, no one else has one exactly like yours. Just look at your fingerprint! Really, look at it right now. Even though it looks like any other fingerprint at first, it's not and there is no other match in the world. That's what I loved about these guys, they understood this as surfers while the rest of our culture seemed to try and look, think, and talk alike.

So the first morning on our surf trip down in Malibu was sweet. The waves were only about waist high, but it was a windless warm morning. Jeff and I were walking up the lower sandy point and talking about the contest, when we saw this beginner riding the whitewater of the wave as he was struggling on his knees trying to stand up on his surfboard. The guy fell off of his board and washed up onto the high tide shore break right in front of us. Suddenly Jeff ran full speed at him, and my immediate thought was, "Is he going to heckle this guy?"

Jeff grabs the guy, walks up the steep sandy shoreline holding him in a head lock! Jeff was a tough guy who knew how to fight, so my thoughts were "What did this guy do?"

So he walks up to me with a smile on his face as if he'd found a bag full of a million dollars. So this poor guy's face is turning red but Jeff was oblivious to it and continues to smile ear to ear. Suddenly he shouts to me, "George, look at who I've got. Its _____". It was a famous movie star, even to this day.

Then he orders me, "Get my camera, take a picture of us".

I got his camera and he had me take a few pictures of them together, the movie star with an uncomfortable looking red face in Jeff's embracing headlock. Jeff's smile grew and he shouted out his name again for the whole beach to hear.

Suddenly Skin Dog came running down the beach and Jeff yelled, "Skinny, look who I've got".

The Hollywood star was actually a humble guy who ended up smiling (after the headlock eased into an arm over his shoulder), he shook hands and talked with us for a while.

After a fun surf in the sun splashed glassy four foot waves we were hungry. So we piled into Jeff's rusty pickup truck and headed down the Coast Highway looking for a place to eat.

Jeff's truck was a classic beat up surfer's ride. He had his surfing sponsors' stickers placed all over the back window. Melted surfboard wax stains were all over the hood and bed. But what was unique to Jeff was the massive pile of decomposing banana peels laid out on the dashboard. Some still yellow, some brown, and many black and shriveled up. When we started our trip Jeff was preaching to me about how you can live healthy on just banana's and water.

So we found a fancy burger restaurant right off of the

Coast Highway. The minute we walked in I was nervous about how much our bill was going to be. This place had numerous photos on the wall signed by famous Hollywood celebrities.

We were seated down in the center of the restaurant at a large table covered with a bright white table cloth. The waitress walked over filling our tall glasses with iced water and fresh lemons followed by a large basket of steaming hot, fresh baked bread along with real butter on a fancy dish.

The second she left our table we started ripping into the bread and butter. We ate all of the warm bread by the time she came back. The young waitress was surprised and her eyes bulged wide open in shock as she said, "Oh my, I will get another basket for you guys." She came back to our table with our second helping of steamy fresh baked bread. Then she gently laid down the thick artistically designed menus in front of each of us.

We drank down our ice cold lemon water, opened up our menus and noticed the hamburgers started at $22.oo. Jeff slammed the menu shut looked at all of us and locked his stare at Skinny and began his loud trade mark laugh: "Arr, Arr, Arr, Arr, Arr!" The whole restaurant stopped eating and starred at us. Suddenly Skinny made eye contact with Jeff and joined him with a louder: "Arr, Arr, Arr, Arr. Then I joined in: "Arr, Arr, Arr, Arr".

This laugh was just "Out of the blue", spontaneous, facetious, craziness as we all got up and laughed the ridiculous "Arr, Arr, Arr, right out of the restaurant.

Looking back on that classic scene, I realize it was good enough for a Hollywood movie.

The rest of the day was all about finding a place to stay. After all, we slept in the back Jeff's pickup truck parked in a parking lot on the way down.

So "Skinny" and Jeff looked for and found the most beautiful girls on Malibu beach. They boldly sat next to them, made them laugh a few times and just like that, we had a place to stay. Not only did we have a place to stay, but this was a Malibu mansion overlooking the Ocean. We had our own guest house with a large Jacuzzi pool and we for the entire three-day contest.

This is how I remember these surf trips. They were spontaneous and full of fun. There was never a dull moment as every hour became a new adventure.

Santa Cruz had a large group of highly talented young

surfers. I am so stoked to have been a part of those guys. Surfing every day at the best spots with guys like: Josh Mulcoy, Peter Mel, Adam Replogle, Jason "Rat boy" Collins, Chris Gallagher, Justin Burns, Ken "Skin Dog" Collins, Shawn "Barney" Barron, Darryl "Flea" Virostko, and many more.

In Santa Cruz there were three high schools and they all had surf teams.

Harbor high was where I went my freshman year, and this was where the mid-town locals went. Some great surfers came out of that school such as: Josh Mulcoy, who by the way made the cover of Surfer magazine from a photo taken in Alaska recently, while I was writing this book.

Santa Cruz high was where the Westside locals went with a powerful crew of surfers such as: Jason "Rat boy" Collins, Darryl "Flea" Virostko, Shawn "Barney" Barron, and many more.

Last but not least was Soquel High School. This was primarily the Eastside locals and was where I ended up going as a sophomore and senior. We had "Frosty" as our surf team coach and we had some serious talent.

The Same Today

Our High School Surf Team with "Frosty" our coach.

Some of my High School surf buddies

Jeff Lansing

This is me at 17 years old, surfing just north of Santa Cruz.

My Water Color Painting of the point.

The surf where I live now

My friend Adam Replogle went on to the World Tour as a professional surfer and won a few of those contests. Kieran Horn became a pro as well, and also won a few including the "Cold Water Classic". Justin Burns had serious talent who was way ahead of its time. He surfed just like the best guys do today and I believe he was capable of being in the top ten of the world.

We had the best surf coach, "Frosty". He later mentored the legendary big wave rider, Jay Moriarity. I remember him as a tough coach who used to say often, "You need to be here now"!

Ironically Jay's wife Kim was my next door neighbor during high school. I remember her and her little brother would walk down to my house to look for their cat named "Goatee" who was always sleeping on the wood porch of my home.

Those were the days – surf all the time with my friends while receiving free surf gear.

The surfer crowd at my high school was made up of some macho guys. We were by no means politically correct. We liked to surf gnarly waves, take risks, and fight. We were the only group of students who had the guts to tell our politically correct, public school staff exactly what we thought of their "crap".

Most of my female teachers in high school seemed to have a deep rooted bitterness toward men. One of my teachers who was a U.C. Santa Cruz graduate had a clear agenda to rewrite history according to her view of it. She might as well have called it "Her story" instead of "History". She was supposed to be teaching us history but it was obvious that she taught us partial history.

Miss "Feminazi" spent most of our time focused on how evil the white European, and American men behaved. Ms. "Infallibus Fertilittus" (as I often called her) painted Abraham Lincoln as just another politician who really didn't care about the African American slaves. Ms. "Her story" plunged us right in to how evil white men were to the Native Americans never discussing how evil some of them were to each other. She even talked about her Native lover in the Southwest.

She finally taught her way to World War II and so I thought this might be something good, after all both of my grandpa's served in that war. I knew my grandpa's were men of integrity, and I admired and loved them. So I thought, "Alright, maybe this will be interesting"!

So she starts the class by throwing in a black and white video clip of the end of the war celebrations showing parades, confetti, men and women kissing, and dancing. As we watched the film the commentator announced, "The war is over and now its girls, girls, girls…"

So my teacher shuts the video down, the fluorescent lights flickered on as they illuminated her cold stare. Then she looks at us with monstrous distain in her eyes and announces, "We will not look into World War II at all because it was a bunch of male chauvinist pigs. Instead, we will spend the rest of the semester covering Women's History and African American History".

I looked around the class to see if anyone else was as shocked as I was. But no one seemed to care! It was as if these future adults were a bunch of clones being told what to think, more than how to think.

That moment became the fulcrum, the tipping point of focused direction in my life. Surfing became everything to me and high school became nothing to me. This was because of intellectual bullying. I knew these teachers were teaching partial truths which is the same as teaching a lie. They took on the Nazi tactic of telling a lie over and over until most everyone believes it. So, I mentally shut down to her endless preaching of "Her story, taught her way".

Surfing became my life. At least with surfing it was real! The waves we surfed were tangible, honest, natural, free, organic, and powerful. The surfers were tough, honest, and real. The men who surfed seemed to be the only real men in Santa Cruz at that time. No, they weren't perfect but they were men who knew the value in taking a risk, because they found freedom in the surf.

We survived and mastered the local surf spots while charging powerful waves. We took our time to search for the best waves every chance we got.

Many of us worked construction jobs, and while working we talked about the surf.

Surfing the local contests was always a fun time for us

Santa Cruz locals. We joked with each other, and laughed often. During one of our surf contests at Steamer Lane someone brought boxing gloves and so the mass of young locals shifted from the contest and turned into a large circle around the boxing matches. It got to the point of blocking traffic and so the police put an end to it.

We were having lots of fun but at the same time we were pushing the limits in our surfing.

I loved the sponsored surfer life. I was sponsored by Rip Curl wetsuits, Taylor made Surfboards, and Santa Cruz Surf Shop.

This was the life! Just had to surf a few contests (which were really just fun surf trips) and then get all this free surf gear. Oh, and you were required to surf all the time. How perfect is that? This seemed to be the best life.

I remember it well, a sweet morning of surfing, going home for breakfast and listening for that UPS truck. Once a month the Rip Curl box would arrive with two free wetsuits, rice paper decals, shirts, hats, shorts, sweatshirts, and stickers. This was so rad! They also included the order form for your next shipment of wetsuits of your choice. Then, at the bottom of the box was the invoice that showed zero amount owed.

Yes, this was getting something good that I never deserved or earned. I guess that would be the definition of "Grace".

There was boxes stuffed with free wetsuits, clothing, sunglasses, wax, board bags, it was enough to start a small surf shop. It was all a dream come true to any young surfer.

After competing in the fifth pro surf contest of that year I came to a major turning point in my life. I took last place in my first heat of the contest and was done.

Before the start of the heat I remember standing next to the San Clemente Pier feeling the warm sand between my toes, my surfboard waxed, contest jersey on, and waiting to paddle out at the sound of the buzzer.

My heartbeat was elevated as I watched the surf in hopeful anticipation of surfing well in my heat. As I watched the heat before mine, I realized it was Kelly Slater who was dominating the heat as he found speed and power in the weak two-foot wind slop of waves. Just watching this future world champ surf before me weakened my confidence in my surfing ability. It would be like watching Albert Einstein chalk out a crazy math problem on the board realizing you were next to come up with a brilliant formula.

I totally bombed out in my heat and I was totally bummed out. I surfed worse than I ever had. Every wave I rode felt like I was a day-one beginner because I was unable to produce speed to do any turns.

When the heat ended I knew I was done. I knew that my surfing dreams of being a top pro surfer were over. I swallowed all of my heart breaking emotion, turned in my contest jersey and then drove north as fast as I could.

Taking the Coast Highway up through Malibu I stopped in Ventura. My brother was born in Ventura and my family lived in that beautiful city for few years and so we had family connection there and came to visit them often.

After a grumpy unfulfilling surf in three-foot sunny beach break, I felt like there was a hole in my soul. This would be the opposite feeling of that ultimate surfing experience a year before.

That evening I decided to sleep in the back of my pickup truck. I could have stayed at my friend's house but I wanted to be alone. That night I was parked at a surf spot called "Emma wood" which is a state beach just north of Ventura.

Listening to the surf pound the high tide shore while laying down in back of my pickup truck I realized that night that I needed some serious change in my life.

So that night, at nineteen years old I realized that surfing was not the answer to finding true and lasting satisfaction in life. I remember crying out to God, "Why couldn't I be a pro surfer? So now what? What's my path, what am I meant to be in this life?"

I fell asleep hearing the waves that night as the sound of them faded away. This is what happened in my heart as well. The power of the waves in my life faded away that night.

So I began to surf less and started going to Cabrillo College. It was amazing how I was an "F" student in public high school and never even graduated but was able to go to College.

I loved it. The teaching was so much better than that lame high school. Some of the professors were politically correct but they were still able to teach.

I loved my World Geography Class. The professor of this class was a brilliant teacher. When he taught it was like you were going on an adventure to the outer regions of the world. It was as if we were archeologists exploring Egypt, Morocco, South Africa, Asia, Europe and the Middle East.

He was an amazing teacher as your imagination was

engaged as he turned the words into pictures. Some of the students didn't like his class because they said his final exam was too hard. He told us to do the reading and studying and the final test won't be a problem. I listened to him and did what he said.

The final exam was mostly essay answers and he graded all exams on a curve. A bunch of the students dropped the class in fear of the grade curve.

The final exam was easy for me because I loved the class so much. I was so excited and anxious to see my grade.

The last day came and he passed our graded exams out to us. Some students were sighing and some sighed in relief. Mine came and there it was at the top of the exam booklet, 189/200, an A+ because he graded on the curve.

"I got an A on a College Final Exam", I whispered with a growing smile. I was so happy.

I honestly thought I was stupid and had no chance at anything in life. But now things were different, because I got an excellent grade. The professor told me later that I actually had the highest score he ever had for that final exam. Wow, what a confidence booster.

I still didn't know if four years of college was for me. I

thought about serving my country and earning college money at the same time. It was a "no brainer". Plus, I needed to get out of Santa Cruz and see the real America.

One day I was at home feeling a bit purposeless while slumped on the couch with the TV remote in hand. I remember watching the Discovery channel and there it was, a documentary on the "Best Ranger Competition". As I watched these tough men complete, I knew that was what I needed to do.

I went to the recruiter and told him I wanted to be an Army Ranger.

He asked me if I had graduated from High School. I said, "No, but I am a full time college student."

He said sorry you still must have a high school diploma. I couldn't believe it. So I made some phone calls and figured out that I had to go to the Santa Cruz High School Adult education class.

This was humbling for me and that was a good thing. So after a few adult classes and tests it was done. Diploma in hand I signed up for the Army with a guarantee to go to Airborne School and to try out as an Airborne Ranger.

The Same Today

Chapter Four: Ranger

Basic training was long and repetitive. I was glad it was over and somehow by God's grace I was made honor graduate.

Now it was off to Airborne School. This school was full of a lot of hype. The students were motivated to earn their "Jump Wings". It was just more training to me, I didn't really care about the parachuting or earning the airborne badge. I just wanted to make it to the Rangers.

Early in the morning we would run four to five miles singing Airborne cadence. I remember thinking, "Can't we just run without all the cadence singing and marching"? Then I noticed small groups of tough looking men wearing all black running clothes. These guys were in three to eight man groups and they were running at a faster pace. They weren't singing cadence songs and they couldn't because they were breathing too heavy.

I asked the guy next to me who those guys were, and he said, "Those are the Ranger Battalion boys". I was in awe of them and I also thought it was smart to run like that because that's how they would run in combat. No one is going run in formation, singing songs in the heat of battle.

Finally, Airborne school was over. Three weeks of training and five jumps and we were finally done.

The graduation ceremony was like all of the rest of the military ceremonies. A commanding officer gives a long speech while we all stood in the position of attention with many passing out from standing in the humid Georgia heat.

After the big ceremony, we were marched back to the Airborne School Barracks. There was much celebrating and picture taking with family members and friends but it was just another school to me.

Slowly the barracks emptied. It was strange because the once crowded building was like a ghost town.

I headed down to the headquarters office and asked the cadre when I was going to the Ranger Indoctrination Course (RIP) and what to expect.

The First Sergeant came out of his office and looked at me with a certain respect for me because I was volunteering for this. He then gave me a bunch of good information.

He said, "Go get all your gear in your army issued duffle bag and get outside front in the formation area. While waiting have your ID badge, dog tags, and orders in a zip lock bag. Drink lots of water, don't say anything to the Ranger Cadre and whatever you do, do not and I repeat, do not wear an airborne beret. They will show up sometime this afternoon and will run you up to five miles while you carry everything you own. So, get ready and good luck to you".

I took what he said seriously and headed straight to my wall locker and packed. I filled up my two-quart canteen with water and headed downstairs and outside into the formation area. So there I was, by myself standing next to my gear dressed in my battle fatigue uniform with the standard camo patrol cap on.

Then one of the graduated students walked by me asking what I was doing so I told him I was waiting for the Rangers to show up. He looked a bit surprised and said he was going too. So he ran to get his stuff, got into uniform and stood next to me. I looked at him and said, "Get rid of that beret and put your patrol cap on". He told me thanks and got rid of it.

Slowly some of the others came back from celebrating. They were a mix. Some wearing their civilian clothes, and others still in uniform but with Airborne Beret's on. I told them to get ready, and some of them seemed a bit arrogant about what I told them.

We stood there for a few hours because they could have shown up at any time. The afternoon shadows began to show and many of the men waiting were laying down on their gear. Some were smoking cigarettes, some were wearing board shorts and flip flops.

Suddenly out of nowhere three men wearing the Ranger black berets showed up. They immediately started screaming at the guys lying down, "Get the hell up, now, you dirt bags."

Then they walked up to the guys wearing the Airborne Berets and grabbed them off of their heads and threw them across the courtyard. One guy protested, "Hey that's mine". They ignored him and said, "Get your gear on now, all of you".

Then up in the barracks' third floor a young soldier shouted out the window, "I am supposed to go to RIP too, wait for me."

One of the Rangers ran up into the barracks and all we

heard was screaming and doors slamming. A few minutes later this poor guy was walking over to us with eight bags of stuff he had accumulated. He was struggling to carry it all and the Rangers told him, "You shouldn't have bought all that worthless crap from the commissary you fool." Then the senior Ranger shouted out, "Let's move out".

We ran fast. We ran and we ran, sweating profusely and breathing heavy. It was very hot and humid on this day.

We ran passed the Ranger Regiment Headquarters Building which had a huge satellite dish next to it. Then we ran through the gates and passed the large fenced-in compound.

They ran us in and had us drop everything to the gravel-covered ground. Then they immediately made us do pushups as they walked into their barracks. After about ten minutes we were struggling just to hold the push up position.

Then one of them came out and yelled, "drink water". We drank all the water we had. Then he took roll call and had us file in to the barracks. There were no assigned bunks, no issued bunk sheets or blankets like all the other courses in the Army. The Rangers did not waste time on traditional military things like making your bunk perfect, shining your boots or putting your locker in perfect order.

So I went in and luckily found a bottom bunk.

Then we were waiting for whatever was next, when suddenly the senior Ranger came upstairs and told us we were free for the weekend. He said the course was to begin Monday at O' Five-hundred. So just like that it was over for a couple of days.

This two-day delay until the course started was great for gathering info on what to expect from the failures who were waiting to recycle into another class. They were staying in the barracks from the last class and so they gave a lot of good tips.

Monday came quickly and the next few weeks were "Hell Weeks".

The instructors were all Ranger Battalion combat veterans of the Grenada, and Panama operations.

These guys were like nothing I had seen in the Army so far. They were lean and mean. They were very serious and tough. I later found out that two of the instructors were just weeks away from going to Delta Force so they were in top physical shape. They seemed to use our class to train up for their next unit which made things tough on our class.

After seventy-two hours of grueling physical training it

felt so bad that you wanted quit the whole time. Our uniforms were dripping wet from sweat so much we looked like we just swam through the swamp.

Then they ran us to a large field about three football fields long and one of the future Delta Force Rangers said, "Bear crawl to the end of the field and back".

I thought, "You have to be kidding me, I feel like falling over and dying from exhaustion and he wants us to bear crawl that far"?

We started in and the entire field was covered in sharp hardened grass spurs. These thorns would stick into your hands and they hurt. But that pain quickly left as the throbbing pain of bear crawling kicked in. I was just at the tail end of the first of three groups who made it down and all the way back when the instructor stood in front of me and said, "Starting with you and everyone behind you, do it again".

This tweaked with my mind. I couldn't believe this. As I turned around I saw collapsed guys all across the entire field. I knew this was impossible but I somehow made my mind overcome everything and just grew numb to the pain and somehow made it again.

At the end of this brutal bear crawl, a whole group of

guys volunteered to quit. This group of guys got to watch the rest of us get "Smoked" for another two hours before stopping. It was non-stop pushups, bear-crawling, crab-walking, and leg-lifts. When we stopped for a short time to drink water I saw that the group of quitters was five times the size as it was before.

Right after this, we had to run ten miles in the middle of the hot June day. But this wasn't just any ten mile run because we had to carry a stretcher with a guy on it and if you weren't doing that, you were carrying a five gallon can full of water. This was a "hell run" that got worse and worse.

The instructors began to harass us more and more. One instructor yelled out, "I'm going to beat the hell out of anyone who crosses the double yellow line again." I didn't think he really meant it. But then I heard some yelling behind our group carrying the stretcher and it was that instructor kicking one of the young guys who crossed the double yellow.

When this run ended I realized this was not a game anymore. These guys were dead serious about all of this. I felt like Basic Training and Airborne School were just a game you played to graduate and be done. But this was different. These guys weren't playing; this was for real.

We suffered nonstop for three weeks straight. We got little to no sleep, hardly had a chance to eat, and carried lots of weight.

We started with around two-hundred men and ended with just twenty-nine; Keep this in mind, these were all motivated men who were in excellent shape.

Of those twenty-nine, only half lasted the first couple of weeks in their assigned Ranger Battalion. Of those, only a few of us made it three to four years. Just a few of us graduated from Ranger School and became Ranger Sergeants.

The grueling Ranger Indoctrination Course was over and the day came for the six of us who were assigned to 3rd Ranger Battalion to march over to our new home. Third Battalion was right next to the 75th Ranger Headquarters where we had our Ranger Indoctrination Course.

We were all scared. We heard nothing but horror stories about how bad we would be treated for our first couple of years in the unit.

As we marched over, we were led over by Master Sergeant Lamb who was a seasoned combat veteran with Special Forces. Then we were marched right in front of the entire Charlie Company Rangers and they were all geared up carrying weapons for training.

They hooted and hollered at us, "Oh yeah I get that one with the shiny boots and pressed uniform. You won't be dressing like that anymore boy", another one yelled, "What are you looking at dirt bag? I hope your assigned to this company so I can smoke you".

As we marched passed we knew we were in for it. We went straight to the admin office to in-process. They made us sit in these ridiculously small desks and fill out paperwork. Then one of the office Rangers said, "Ok, now you just need to wait for your Team leaders to come and get you and I advise you to drink water."

So we waited for about twenty minutes when suddenly the door burst open. "Where is he" yelled out a young angry Sergeant with a tall skinny Corporal right behind him. The admin guys pointed him out and they both got in his face examining him from about three inches away. The Corporal said, "I don't like you and I don't think you're going to make it here".

They screamed at him to get all his crap and get out the door. The rest of us heard him doing pushups and other drills just outside the office for what seemed like an hour.

Then another Sergeant came in. This guy wasn't the loud obnoxious type like the other two but seemed overly serious. He called out the name of his new Ranger and he stood to his feet quivering and shaking in fear. The older sergeant walked up to him and yelled out, "Relax". This only made it worse as he fumbled with his gear and headed out the door.

Four of us were remaining, and the door burst open again. By this time the admin leader named Sergeant Cajun had enough of his door being slammed open so he yelled out, "I'm going to kill the next guy that slams that door open."

The two young Sergeants burst in, paced back and forth and one of them yelled out, "Which ones are mine"? One of them had to be the ugliest guy I had ever seen. As I looked closer I saw that he was actually drooling out of his mouth. He looked us all over with a vindictive smile and crazy eyes. Then he started breathing heavy again and saliva mixed with foamy bubbles appeared out of the corner of his mouth. I felt sorry for the two guys that went with them.

After those two left like hungry lions with their fresh meat, a calm yet fierce looking older Sergeant came in and said, "Which one of you is Crabb?" I stood up and shouted,

"Here Sergeant".

He calmly said, "Get you gear and let's go".

He didn't say a word to me and led me to our company barracks. He told a young private to get me a room and wall locker on the third floor. I learned later that he had just been accepted into Delta Force.

This was tough stuff being in the Rangers. Our training alone was extremely dangerous. During my three and a half years there, twelve Rangers were killed in training alone. Among those who died was First Sergeant Harris who was in the battle of Mogadishu, Somalia, and a year later he parachute landed in the Chattahoochee River at night and drowned. Then after I graduated Ranger School, five West Point graduates died of hypothermia in the same school.

One night five Rangers were seriously injured and one died in a fast roping accident. The Louisiana treetops looked like grass in the darkness of night but trees were over ninety feet tall and so they fell and one was killed by hanging from his harness. Another young Ranger died only after two weeks of being in the Battalion because a piece of concrete flew up in the air after setting off a Claymore Mine and cut open his Femoral Artery.

I remember my first parachute jump in the Rangers.

I was only in the unit two days.

It was a night time, full combat load tactical jump out of a C-130 aircraft. I was already a nervous wreck being the new Ranger and this night jump was scary stuff.

My team leader, Sergeant Hayes, was a wild country boy from the South. He told me to find another Private to help me get "Squared away" with all of my gear for that night's full combat load parachute jump and so I did what I was told.

Then Sergeant Hayes came in and told me to follow him. He took me back over to his see his old Platoon Sergeant who was leaving that day for Delta Force.

We arrived to the steps of Charlie company barracks and there he was, Staff Sergeant Busch. Sergeant Hayes asked him a bunch of questions about Delta selection and then shook his hand congratulating him on making it.

I noticed something peculiar about him. His presence seemed different than the others. He seemed to have a peace about him, a certain goodness about his spirit.

I learned later that he was a strong believer in Jesus Christ. He used to tell his worried mother, "Don't worry about me mom, I'm just one click away from heaven."

I also found out later that he was the first of the Delta

Force operators killed in Somalia just a few months later.

Now it was time for our nighttime, full-combat-load parachute jump with my new leader Sergeant Hayes.

He sat across from me on the aircraft and kept saying, "I'm going to get you boy". He made sure he sat across from me as the fifth jumper on the opposite side so that we would end up near each other when our chutes opened.

Then the side door was opened and the aircraft was dark. All you could see was the slightly less dark opening of the door. Then the call for, "Stand up" was shouted out. Standing with the hundreds of pounds of equipment pulling you down was a horrendous task alone. Then the call for ten minutes, one minute, thirty seconds, go! Just like that the line moved forward in the darkness toward the roaring sounds of the engines.

I remembered everything I was taught in Airborne School but this was way different. This was much tougher. Finally, I reached the door and jumped feeling the freefall and wash of the prop blast spinning me around.

Finally, my chute opened and that sudden peaceful silence filled the air. I quickly checked the chute and looked around for other jumpers to avoid.

Suddenly I heard the familiar sound of Sergeant Hayes's

voice. "I'm going to get you Crabb. Ha, ha here I come", he shouted this with an arrogant laugh to it.

I saw him pull his right side riser toggle as steered his parachute right at me then he yelled, "I'm going to get you Crabb". I tried to steer away from him but he seemed to come directly at me as he was about forty feet higher and to my left.

Laughing loudly, he flew right underneath me and I yelled out, "What are you doing? We're going to get killed".

Suddenly my parachute lost all of its form and collapsed. I was free falling again as I saw him flash by at a high rate of speed. After a few long seconds of this my chute fully opened again. I knew right away what was happening. We were stealing each other's air. This means we were so close that the void of air left in your wake causes the other chute to collapse and you freefall. This is hard to get out of because it was like a vortex that keeps pulling you back in.

I frantically tried to pull right and get away from him but we were both in this hopeless trap of stealing each other's air.

The end result of this scenario is one of us was going to

land very hard and get hurt or killed.

I remember praying a desperate prayer for help. "Lord, please help; this is not good Lord. Please help".

After a few times of stealing each other's air, I remember landing softly. This was by far the softest landing I had ever had in all of my parachute jumps.

I laid there and thanked God.

Then I heard a loud "Thump" followed by screaming.

"Oh no, Sergeant Hayes", I thought.

I unclipped and ran over to where he was. I was scared for him because his screaming was becoming louder and louder. The medics were there immediately and got him on a backboard. We were all told by the Medic in-charge to get our gear and head over to the bus.

As I got on the bus it seemed like every Ranger started yelling at me, "What the hell did you do to your Sergeant, your cherry piece of crap"? I found a seat and one of them told me to get the hell up and do pushups.

The whole way back to our Ranger compound I was in the pushup position with guys yelling and throwing things at me. We got back to the compound and the First Sergeant said that Hayes broke his tail bone.

I was immediately relieved that it wasn't more serious

but still sad about the whole thing.

So I didn't start off on the best foot in Ranger Battalion, but changes were in the air. Just a couple of weeks later the entire unit headed out for Joint Special Operations Training down near El Paso, Texas. We jumped into the desert north of El Paso, Texas.

We were here to train with the other elite units such as Delta Force and Seal Team Six. There were also a few Special Operations Israeli soldiers onsite with their General.

These training missions were so dangerous. One night we were training to seize and airfield and the planes all landed by night vision with all lights off. There was literally no light on the desert airstrip except for the distant city lights of El Paso. The thunderous roar of shadowy aircraft filled the night air.

As the tactical cargo aircraft landed and slowed down the rear ramps would open downward onto the tarmac and the Ranger vehicles and motorcycles would offload followed by the men on foot.

As the Rangers ran off of the paved tarmac and into the night time desert, they got into the prone position, laying down concealed by the grass and cactus.

Right after that, another aircraft offloaded and the jeeps drove off by night vision only. The drivers that headed south were blinded by the distant glowing lights of the city. The night vision devices just made it worse. One driver couldn't see and instead of stopping and having someone ground-guide him at a jogging rate of speed, he decided to just drive blind.

He ran over a Ranger Captain who was lying in the prone position. His jeep was a half a second away from running over the Israeli General who rolled out of the way just in time.

The Captain lived but was paralyzed. This is how dangerous this Ranger Battalion training was.

The next day we headed out for some explosives training. As soon as we arrived the instructors were putting their finishing touches on their C-4 plastic explosives creations. They sculpted a rabbit and a car out of the plastic explosives as if it were just play doe.

When the class began they lit both sculptures on fire and said this stuff also makes a great fire starter but don't try to stomp it out or, "Bang". They explained it takes pressure and heat to set off the plastic explosives.

We got to blow a bunch of stuff up that day and it was a

whole lot of fun.

I met a young Hispanic Ranger named Sergeant Ruiz. He had a twelve-gauge shotgun slung over his back. He was a warm and genuine guy who just loved being an Army Ranger.

While we were training for a real world scenario to fight terrorism, Bravo company was gathered up and taken away to train with Delta at their secret compound.

Our second in command took the rest of us out a quarter of a mile into the desert and told us that Bravo company is heading to Somalia. He said the rest of us will be joining them shortly. Then a big smile stretched across his face followed by a head tilting spit from his chewing tobacco filled mouth. After he spit he said, "We're going kick some Somali ass, boys".

In response to that comment the whole group of Rangers yelled out, "Hooaah".

It seemed a bit arrogant to me because only days earlier I played the bad guy on one of the downed black hawk training missions and I realized how easy it would be to kill a whole squad as they descended down the fast ropes.

So the B Company boys were heading to Somalia with Delta Force. These men were the same guys who were portrayed in the movie, "Blackhawk Down".

They came back changed men. Many of them personally told me detailed accounts of what happened on October 3rd. Sometimes they were angry, other times they were tearing up as they recalled their brother's screams of pain in those dusty, blood-stained streets of Somalia.

One story stuck with me over the years. It was about the two Delta Force Operators named Gordon and Randy.

These two men were in a helicopter during the October 3rd battle. Their assigned task was sniper support hovering above the mission location.

After the second Black Hawk helicopter was hit and crashed, all of the other helicopters were ordered to move to a higher elevation out of range of the rockets. Some of the Somalis modified their Rocket Propelled Grenade launchers so they were able to shoot an air-burst at the helicopters.

The two Delta men could hear over the communications that there was a survivor down below at the second crash site. The problem was there were just enough Rangers to secure the first crash site so the second was left vulnerable. The heavily armed and angry Somalis were starting to flood into the second crash.

These two Delta snipers weren't going to hover above and listen to their defenseless friend get killed below. So they requested to be dropped off to help the pilot named Michael Durant, who was still alive.

They knew all hell was breaking loose down below and they loved the hell out of their friend. So after they finally got their request granted by the General, they were hastily dropped off down below.

The mob below had an unquenchable thirst for blood. This is partly because they had a wrath against these foreign forces. Only weeks before a U.S. Army attack helicopter shot a missile into the wrong building and many of these people found many of their bloodied loved ones dead.

These two Delta Force warriors were innocent of that mistake and by all rights they could stay up above out of harm's way. But, they willingly came down to die in order to give their friend a chance to live.

They began to take the attention off of their friend as they became the focus of the wrath-filled mob. They secured their friend away from the crash, gave him a weapon and went back to the downed Blackhawk to fight. The situation was bad for Gordon and Randy as they fought their last few bullets.

Randy's best friend Gordon was hit and wounded. Then he was hit again and again until he was dead.

Randy ran back to Durant and gave him his pistol with his last few rounds and told him, "Gordy's gone".

Then Randy ran back to the crash site where his fallen comrade laid. He fought his best all the way to his last bullet, but was overwhelmed by the hundreds of armed Somalis, and was killed too.

Those two men became the focus and satisfaction of the mob's wrath. They were absorbing the hell that their friend was destined to have and it's because they "Loved the hell out of their friend".

Mike Durant knows this great love that these brothers in combat had for him. He retells the story with tears in his eyes because of those two elite warriors who sacrificed themselves for him.

I was reading a scripture out of the book of 1st John that described this very same kind of thing. He was one of Jesus' closest friends on earth and this is what he penned, "He himself is the propitiation for our sins, and not for ours only but also for the whole world" (1st John 2:2).

That word, "Propitiation" is defined as God's righteous

wrath being satisfied by Jesus' sacrifice to save us.

To save us from what?

Our sin.

"What's that?" You might ask.

Sin is something of our nature that all of us humans are born with. It is like when you see a good looking apple but inside you find a worm. That worm was an egg on the blossom before it was ever an apple. So the worm bores and eats its way from the inside out because it was already in the apple. We too are like that apple. We are all bad apples when you get down to the "Core" of it.

The only one in history who never sinned was Jesus. He alone is the perfect "Fruit", so to speak.

Sin is like a Tsunami wave of wrath.

Imagine a wave. There is an invisible force that causes the water to stand up, peak and eventually crash.

Remember the destructive Tsunami's in Indonesia and again, in Japan?

Nothing could stop those monstrous, destructive waves from coming. Well, our sin feeds this huge unstoppable wave of wrath that no one could stop. But there is one who could, and one who did.

His name is Jesus.

Jesus is perfect as a man, and God in one. He came down from the prestige, the luxury and the safety of his home with his Father, that paradise of heaven to rescue us. He saw that we were going to die by the wrath that is coming from our sins. Just like those two elite warriors, those two Delta operators who volunteered to go down into that hellacious crash site in Somalia. In that same way, Jesus came down from heaven to ground level and got shot at – so to speak, by the religious leaders.

Then he blew everyone's mind by grabbing his cross to take on that huge wave of wrath. Imagine it this way, he grabbed his wooden surfboard called the cross holding it tightly. He entered the water and made it out to exactly the right spot at the right time and by his power paddled into and caught that huge wave of wrath, fed by our sins.

He dropped into the most giant, ugly, destructive tsunami of a wave that there ever was. He rode that wave of sin on his cross and was consumed by it. The huge vortex tunnel of death ate him. All of his friends lost hope.

But then three days later that black hole of death could not swallow him and had to spit him out. So that wave of death spits him out and he conquered death once and for all.

Jesus said it himself, "As Jonah was three days and three nights in the belly of the great fish, so will the Son of Man (Himself) be three days and three nights in the heart of the earth."

He did it because there was no other way and he did it because he loves you. You! Not just for the whole world but personally for you.

So Jesus surfed into the deepest, darkest, pit of wrath and was spit out. He became the propitiation for us!

So my Ranger brothers came home changed from Somalia. Six dead, many disabled, and all of them had post-traumatic stress. I remember many of them were waking up in the middle of the night screaming.

Because of the injuries there were a bunch of openings to go to Ranger School. Ranger school was an intense course of seventy-two days if you made it straight through. Most Rangers fail a phase or two and had to recycle the phase so it took a lot longer than seventy-two days.

One guy spent over a whole year in Ranger school. He recycled time after time then made it to the very end and failed the last patrol. So he had to go all the way back to the beginning in Fort Benning, Georgia.

Ranger school is not what made you a real Ranger any more than going to any school makes you what your studying to be. Many of the real Rangers in our Ranger unit never went to Ranger school and never needed to. They could have taught most of the instructors at Ranger school better tactics.

It's like a man who goes to Seminary school to be a pastor-preacher and teacher. Many of these guys who graduated with honors at these schools are not always the best Bible teachers. These guys rely on their education and not the power of God to give a message and so they put their congregation to sleep. Then a guy with no formal education but who has studied the Bible, and is gifted by God to teach and preach is much more qualified than the educated man.

Never the less, Ranger school was made an important part of the Ranger Battalions if you wanted to become a leader. Most guys who graduated became Sergeants within just one year.

My leader, Sergeant Hayes, came in one morning with a smile on his face and said, "I have great news for you. I am sending you to Ranger School. Fear fell over me as he finished that sentence.

I gulped and asked, "When will I go, Sergeant"?

He said, "In one week".

I hadn't been in the Ranger battalion for more than six months and I was being sent to Ranger school? This was ludicrous.

So I began to prepare for Pre-Ranger course. This course was required for all Ranger battalion guys so that the Ranger unit could weed out the guys who might embarrass the 75th Rangers.

This Pre-Ranger School course was tough.

It was December and it was cold. The instructors were all combat veterans who have never been in any other unit but the Ranger battalion. One of them was just getting ready to move up into Delta Force and he loved to take us on hellacious long runs.

We were out in the December cold with no fire and wet uniforms. My uniform was frozen crunchy solid one morning as I had to get it on for the early morning run. We got about one hour of sleep if we were lucky. I also had blisters under blisters and had to run ten miles without using my heals. So the cold combined with running on my toes caused some hellacious cramps in my calves.

One morning around 4 am they made us all low crawl

with our faces in the frozen frosty grass. Some guys started to lift their heads up a bit because of the icy grass. They were singled out and the instructors stepped on and smashed their shoes on their heads to force them back down.

We had days upon days of land navigation training. This is where you were given a compass, protractor, and a map then given grid coordinate numbers that you plotted on the map. Then we were taken way out in the thick woods of Georgia where we were dropped off and let loose by ourselves to find all of the points.

This was tough stuff. I remember it took all night to find these points and it was exhausting. One of the nights I lost my map. This was nearly impossible to do because they had a dummy cord around your neck tied to the map but it must have got caught in all of the thick brush I was busting through, because I lost my map.

The instructor at our base camp almost failed me and kicked me out when I arrived at 4:30 in the morning. Instead he just made me do about an hour of pushups, low crawling, and words of humiliation in front of the whole class.

Later that afternoon we were dropped off by ourselves

again. It was late in the winter afternoon, around an hour before sundown. The instructor yelled out my number and I jumped out of the back of the jeep.

The jeep drove away further up the hill and I could hear the diesel engine fade away up the hill to drop off the remaining three Rangers.

I walked toward the pine tree-filled wood line feeling low, sunken down and depressed. I was thinking of how I wasn't cut out to be a Ranger. Most of the other guys were country boys from the south and it was like second nature for them to do this stuff.

Feeling more and more hopeless, I walked over to the base of a pine tree and "took a knee". My eyes began to well up. I was in deep thought and so I began to talk to God, "Is this all a mistake Lord? I don't think I was cut out for this stuff. I feel like a complete failure God. Please help me to know what I should do."

After a time of silence in sadness and discouragement I stood to my feet and turned around.

I was surprised to see a strong tough looking man standing about five feet away from me looking right at me. He was dressed in "Olive Drab" green which was the old school Army Ranger uniform. He had a patrol cap on with the "Ranger" tab patch sewn on the front. He had dark hair and stood about six foot four.

I thought he was part of the cadre and so I said, "Hey Sergeant". He just looked at me and smiled really big.

Then I looked closer and noticed no rank or name tag on his uniform. As I looked he was like a statue with his eyes focused on me and he just continued to smile.

At this point I was getting a little freaked out and thought he was a crazy guy who dressed up in old Ranger garb and stalked Rangers students. So I walked away from him about ten feet and turned around and he was in that same position with his hands on his hips with a big smile on his face.

Now, I got about thirty feet away and looked back and he was gone, just vanished out of sight. Then I started to wonder, "Who was that guy? Was he an angel sent from God to encourage me?"

That very night I did well. I found all of my points and had the peace of God in my heart.

Three weeks later Ranger school started and I was fortunate to become buddies with a Ranger Battalion guy like me, except for the fact that he had way more experience. Together, we made it straight through the course with no recycles. This was a miracle in and of itself and I know God had his hand in it.

This is all because the Lord is the same yesterday, today, and forever. He was there in ancient times with Joseph. He was there with Elijah, encouraging him when he was depressed and ready to give up. He was there with a common guy like me as well.

Does this mean we should look for God's miracles and angels all the time like many crazy Christians do today?

No.

We don't seek miracles but we should seek the One who sends the miracles. It's up to him if, and when they will appear to us. Who should we look for? His name is Jesus.

Ranger School was tough but I made it. I was the Charlie Company First Sergeant during the course even though I was only a Private First Class.

Graduating Ranger School was a surreal experience. Most of the guys had their wives or dad's there to pin the Ranger tab. I had my tab in my hand but no one was there to pin it on. So suddenly I saw my team leader, Sergeant Hayes. He gave me a firm hand shake and a man hug with a big smile on his face.

He asked me, "Would you like me to pin your Ranger

tab on?"

"I would be honored", I said to him.

This brought great joy to my soul that day. It was awesome.

So about five months later I was promoted to Sergeant.

As the time passed, my Ranger buddy Mike and I, started surfing down in Florida every chance we got. We would drive down to Cocoa Beach Florida and surf Satellite Beach and Sebastian Inlet. We had loads of fun surfing and hanging out with some of the locals down there.

My Ranger buddies and I would also go to the city of Atlanta to party. I was starting to drink too much and go to places where I knew I shouldn't.

We partied all night in Atlanta going from club to club. As the club we were at was giving its last call, we asked some girls where we could find a place that was open. They told us about a club that literally stays open all night and since it was about 2am we headed for that club.

I wasn't really having any fun. This was just a way of trying to hook up with girls. It was undoubtedly the wrong place to look for any girl for a relationship. So, there we were drinking all night and trying to be cool. In the back of my mind I kept wondering what I was doing in these shady bars all through the night. I knew I was in rebellion against my God.

We walked outside of the all-night club and the sun was out. It was 8:30am and we were still a bit drunk.

Lopez was driving and so the three of us jumped in his vintage BMW and started back to Fort Benning. After we got on the Interstate I was beginning to pass out. Lopez said he was good to go and the other guy was already out. So I adjusted the passenger seat back and passed out.

"Watch out", a clear powerful voice spoke into my ear. So I woke up, sat up and looked at Lopez and said. "Watch out". He slowed the car from about 85mph down to 60 and said, "What do you mean watch out?"

"Just watch out", I yelled at him again.

As he slowed down some more, we spotted a pickup truck on the other side of the median spin sideways and cut across the entire median and cut in front of us across all of the lanes in front of us.

Lopez yelled out "Oh no".

We were going slow enough and were aware enough to miss this out of control truck and continue on down the highway.

We both looked at each other and were amazed.

He looked at me again and asked, "How in the hell did you know that was going to happen?"

I said, "Something told me while I was sleeping".

I knew it was the grace of God that saved us from death. I knew that my Lord had intervened on our behalf. But I was still shunning my God even though he was looking after me. I should have boldly announced that it was God who woke me up with those words that saved our lives. But I felt unworthy to announce that after the night of drinking we just had.

The years went by in the Rangers. My best friend, Mike and I ran, swam, and surfed every chance we got. We pushed each other to the limits.

One Saturday morning we decided to run twenty-four miles in the middle of the hot humid Georgia summer day. So we made four of the newer privates set up water stations for us. They weren't too happy about it because it was their day off but we gave them a choice, "Run it with us, or man a water station for us". All four of them chose to man the water station.

Later that year Fort Benning was holding a Triathlon

event. It was a 500-meter swim, fifteen bike, and five mile run. The distances weren't too extreme but the heat index was. It was hot and humid that late morning when it started because it was already 95 degrees with high humidity.

The most elite guys from the 75th Rangers were there to compete. They were known as the RRD - Ranger Reconnaissance Detachment. These guys were the best of the best and many of them move on up into Delta Force.

There were military guys from all over the country in this event. Some of them were sponsored and had five thousand dollar racing bikes.

I had a crappy old ten speed bike, no goggles for swimming, and my Ranger uniform running shorts.

The race started with the swim and it was easy for me because my buddy Mike and I swam almost every day. So I remember finishing first in the swimming part of the event.

The bike part was horrible. The sponsored guys got ahead of me right away. Then some of the elite Rangers passed me.

After the bike ride around the Air Field and through parts of Fort Benning, it was time to run. I rode into the transition zone, and threw my bike down wasting no time to start the run.

By this time the sun was high and it was sweltering hot. The sweat wasn't doing anyone any good because the humidity was so high. It literally felt like the inside of a hot steam room. I started running at a good five-minute mile pace and held it.

Then I saw the two Rangers ahead of me. I was able to overtake them in just a few minutes. After that it was a long hot run and thank God, my friend and I ran in the middle of the day, often. After about twenty minutes I saw one of the sponsored guys. He was about a half of a mile ahead of me in the blazing heat.

The heat got worse and I started to feel dizzy. There was a tingling sensation on the top of my head that felt much like the jaw numbing tingle from eating super-hot peppers. I knew this was getting dangerous but I just kept on running.

I banked around a residential corner and someone there had water cups on a table. I fumbled with the water and got a gulp down. Suddenly I saw one of the two sponsored triathletes. I made it my mission to run him down. As I passed him he sped up and got back in front of me. Then I just held a solid pace and I could see he was hurting from the heat. He soon gave up and fell way back.

After the last turn there was a quarter of a mile straight away. Then I saw the other sponsored guy and he was in first place. I shifted my running up a notch, even though I felt like I was going to pass out the whole time.

As I got closer, within 100 feet he looked back and saw me, then he ran faster. He looked panicked as the finish line was now visible. I caught up to him at about 200 feet from the finish line. He began to sprint and I wasn't going to let him go without a fight so I stayed with him.

Just as we raced about thirty feet to the winner's tape, somehow, some way I dug down deep and shifted my running into an all-out sprint. I quickly passed by him and I could hear him right behind breathing like a panting dog.

Then I went even faster and made a five-foot gap between us and right before my eyes was the finish line. The officials were holding a winners tape up and so I made a fist and punched it as hard as I could. At that moment it seemed like time slowed down, it was like slow motion as the tape ripped in two off of my fist.

People were clapping and smiling. An old man ran up to me and said, "You won Ranger". I couldn't believe it. It was the first time I had won an athletic event.

After shaking hands with the two sponsored guys my

Ranger comrades came in strong. I got to know them and one of them just came back from Delta selection. These guys liked me and told me I should try out for their elite unit.

I started to talk to them about training to do the "Best Ranger Competition". I thought "Why not? I'm in good enough shape to do it". They agreed and so this became the new goal.

When I got back to the Barracks 1st Sergeant Lane was walking up and down the halls with a bull horn in his hand yelling, "Sergeant Crabb where are you? When I find you I am going to kill you.

I got to him and he was in his sweat pants with his hands wrapped for hitting the heavy bag. He looked at me and said, "I am going to kill you and then kick you out of the Rangers unless you have a good reason why you were absent without leave today.

I told him I was in the Fort Benning Triathlon.

He looked at me and started cussing me out.

When he finally finished, I told him that I won.

His "I'm going to kill you" face changed into a warm smile.

He yelled out with his deep scratchy voice, "You won"?

"Hey, Sergeant Crabb won the Triathlon", he yelled out.

"You better have won, you dirt bag", he said smiling at me. Later on he told me that he respected my initiative and backbone because I just went for it in that race.

He was an old school Ranger who loved to yell at us and mess with us all the time.

One time our company went to the super-secret Delta Force compound to do some training. The Delta guys are on a first name basis and very relaxed. Some of the Rangers started relaxing as well by putting their hands in their pockets while hanging around the elite operators. After all this training was the equivalent to James Bond stuff.

First Sergeant Lane wasn't going to have any of this. He ordered the whole company outside and put everyone in the position of attention and had the whole company do pushups while he cussed at us.

The Delta guys were enjoying the show as they watched my whole company being humiliated while they were all laughing. Some of them cheered Lane on by saying, "Good job Bobby! I haven't seen a good old-fashion ass-chewing like that in years."

Later on, during the training one of our Rangers was struck by lightning while on the corner of a roof top. He fell ten feet to the ground. Lane ran over to him and yelled out, "What the hell are you doing laying down? Get up. No, get down and do pushups you dirt bag." The guy started doing pushups and was somehow okay.

These were the kind of days we had in the Ranger Battalion. It was always an adventure with old school guys like Bobby Lane around.

A few months later, First Sergeant Lane and I were in the Ranger Compound Barracks when an older guy with a black cowboy hat and boots walked right up to our steps with a cigarette hanging out of his mouth. He was a tough squinted-eyed, wrinkled face manly-man with hardened features. He looked right through my eyes with his piercing pupils and asked, "Where's your First Sergeant?" At that moment First Sergeant Lane walked out the Barracks door and the stranger yelled out, "Bobby, how the hell are you?"

He was the Delta Force Sergeant Major. He was assigned to be on a training mission that night with our Ranger Unit.

Later that night during the training he got so pissed off at how slow everything was going that he jumped in our hummer and drove it right through our Ranger blocking position. I was riding with him along with members of a unit called Technical Escort. He drove right over the tire spikes and through the razor wire.

This guy was aggressive and he didn't care who disliked it. So we were driving fast through Fort Benning at 3am with razor wire trailing behind us with sparks lighting up the streets. Suddenly the Military Police cars were chasing us with their flashing blue lights ablaze. One of them spoke through the loud speaker, "Pull over now".

The old Delta commando laughed and said, "Where the hell is your Ranger compound, I'm not pulling over for these idiots."

We told him where to turn and the MP's were right on our tail.

He turned into our fenced compound with tires screeching and sparks flying. The MP's stopped outside of it because they were not authorized to come inside. So he drove our Humvee right up onto the grass straddling the sidewalk and punched it right up onto our basketball court in front of our Ranger building.

Within an hour we were all sitting in the meeting room for an after-actions review. This is where we have a big meeting to go over what happened during the training. The problem became obvious immediately. Every officer went up to speak by standing at the position of attention, saluting and saying, "Rangers lead the way Sir". Then they would begin to explain everything they did in a way that was much too traditional. It was far too left brain and ceremonial.

I could see the frustration on the face of the Delta Force Sergeant Major. At the same time First Sergeant Lane bumped my side and laughed and showed me a cartoon he just drew on his note paper. It was a picture of the officer who was up front with a huge light bulb above his head. I couldn't help but laugh.

Then the old Delta Sergeant interrupted the formal Ranger commander mid speech said, "You guys are way too slow. You need to get more aggressive and quit trying to do everything by the book."

One of the Ranger officers glared at him and said, "Who are you? State your name, your rank and address the commander with a formal greeting."

The old, wise, hardened Delta operator shouted, "I am with Delta Force and he's with Seal Team Six. General Downing sent us here to teach you guys. After Somalia we realized your unit is bogged down with too many formalities, rules, and regulations to get the job done."

Then the Seal Team Six Captain spoke up and said, "Speed, is our security".

That night really changed my perspective of the current Rangers that I was a part of.

That night I had a few beers with the Technical Escort Unit guys who came to this training with the Delta and Seal Team Six leaders. These guys told me all about their unit and I became more and more interested.

This unit started out as armed escorts for chemical and biological material being moved from lab to lab across the country. They carried pistols and wore civilian clothing during the escorts. They worked with Delta, Seal Team Six, NSA, CIA, FBI, and the Secret Service on selected missions.

So they gave me their phone number and told me I should join them.

We were scheduled in the Rangers to go to Panama to train in the jungle followed by Canada to train in the winter snow. I didn't want to miss these trips so I waited a couple of months to call the Tech Escort Unit.

We Rangers headed down to Panama with a full combat load and parachuted into the swampy elephant grass. This was a tough parachute jump but we had a lot of fun down there. We trained hard but had some down time as well. We spent eight days in the Jungle and after a while I felt like I was a part of the jungle.

After Panama we had a two week break and we were headed north to Canada. It was in the middle of January and it was icy cold. So we went from hot tropical Central America to sub-zero temperatures of Canada.

We parachuted in the deep snow with mukluk snow boots and snow shoes attached to the rucksacks. One Ranger didn't tie the draw cord tight around his snow boots and when his parachute opened his boots flew off with no chance of recovering them. Lucky for him the track driven snow vehicle was nearby after landing. We had a lot of laughs over this.

We traveled through the deep snow with toboggans and snow shoes in negative sixty below degree weather. We even built snow caves and lived in them. This was a great training experience and we truly enjoyed it.

After these awesome training deployments, I gave Tech Escort a call. After a bit of government paper work, I had my orders to move to my new unit.

They were up in Maryland and so I scheduled a week of leave before heading up to my new unit. I packed up and took off down to Cocoa Beach, Florida to go surfing in the warm water.

I spent five days in the warm sun surfing some fun three to four-foot beach break. I stayed at Patrick Air force base right on the beach. They had awesome motel rooms for only eight dollars a night. The chow hall was like eating at a five-star gourmet buffet. This place was also only a few hundred feet from the beach with great surf.

After relaxing in warm sunny Florida, it was time to hit the road and drive north to Maryland. As I was beginning the journey I had a lot of time to reflect. I was a lonely man at age twenty-five and felt like I needed a wife.

As I was driving, I prayed that God would bring the right woman into my life. Then I felt like he was going to match me up with a woman in Maryland who was His choice for my wife. I just had that knew it in my heart and soul.

After surfing in Virginia Beach, I finally arrived in Maryland.

Technical Escort Unit was a funny place. It was hidden away in these old World War Two era buildings and had a very unique mission.

The unit leadership was happy to see me because I was a

Sergeant from the Ranger battalion. They wanted to get more guys from Special Operations' units to help transform it into a more tactical type of unit.

A few months later, I was in a relationship with a beautiful woman. She was about to graduate from Towson State University and she would later become my bride and my soul mate to this day.

Her name is Christina and I am so thankful to God for bringing us together. One night we talked together all night while our crazed drunk friends partied.

I felt at ease with her. There was something special, and unique about her, as if we knew each other all along. She was an intellectual and our conversations where deep and rich.

At that time I shared a house with two other military guys and one night there was a party. They had hired two strippers to this party. Their plan was to invite all the people they knew and then have the strippers start their act as if they were just some random girls.

Christina and I had a few beers, played pool and socialized a bit during the party. Everything was alright up until the show started.

Immediately I felt a strong nudging in my conscience

and my heart. I knew this was evil and it seemed as if evil was filling the air of that room like a dirty fog. I bent down to talk to Christina and said, "Let's get out of here". Christina strongly agreed with me.

I felt as if all of this dirty foolish living was such a dead end. I knew I was living far away from my God.

So I asked her, "Do you believe in God"?

She said, "Yes, do you"?

I answered, "Yes".

I believe God was watching over us that night.

Later that year we got married. It was the best day of my life and we had an awesome wedding. Her Italian side of the family was great. They are incredible people with strong family values.

My parents were there and danced at the reception with all of their hippie flare. My brother was there with his wife as well. It was a clean wholesome party and the beginning of a new life with my soul mate.

Sergeant Hayes pinned my Ranger Tab on at the graduation ceremony.

Winter training in Canada.

Ranger school graduation picture of us 75th Rangers. I am standing on the far right weighing 130lbs.

Delta Operator Staff Sergeant Busch having some fun in Somalia before he was killed in action on October 3rd.

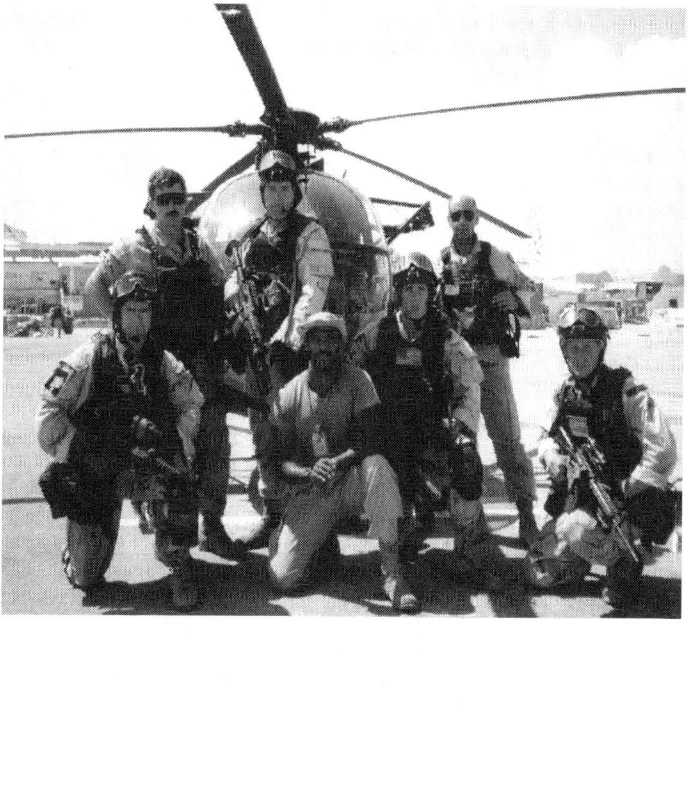

Bravo Company Rangers in Somalia.

Some of my friends who had to run the "Mogadishu Mile" on October 4th.
Five Rangers and two Delta Operators.

This photo was just before transferring to Tech Escort Unit. I had just earned the Canadian Jump Wings (On my right side)

UH – 6 "Little Bird" helicopter rides in New Mexico.

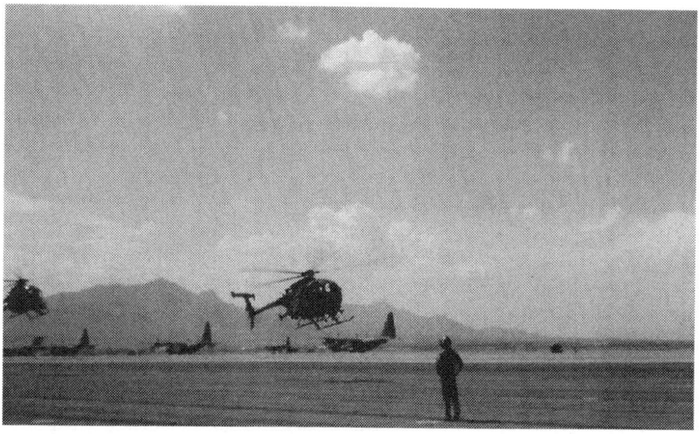

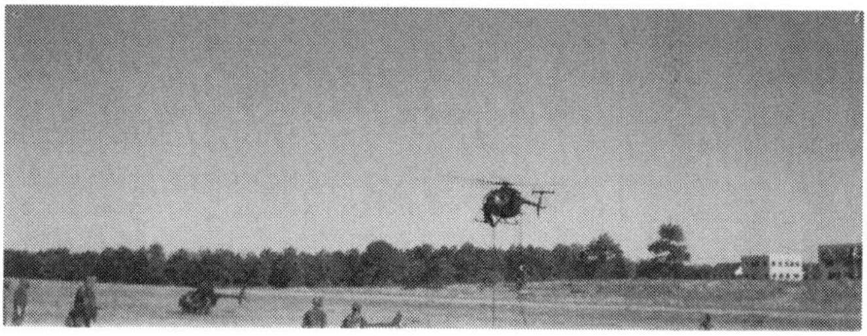

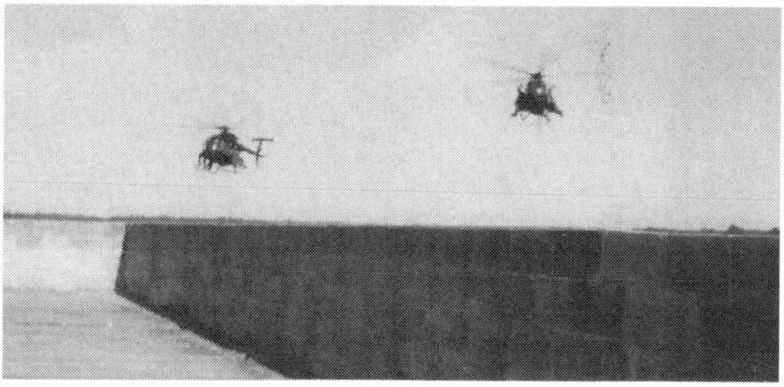

Me and my team after the "Jungle Obstacle Course in Panama. (Middle right)

"One more Ranger!"

My team snow shoeing in Canada. (I am on the far right)

Way below freezing temperatures during our long movement in Canada. We took turns pulling our Toboggan full of survival essentials.

The Same Today

Chapter Five: Grace

My beautiful wife and I were ready to move back to my home town of Santa Cruz, California. It was a great feeling of freedom to be released from the military and move back out West with my bride.

She loved Santa Cruz, from our previous trip, which was for my brother's wedding. So we were excited to start our new life together.

We were lucky to find a place to rent. While I was away serving my country, Santa Cruz was exploding in population. UCSC (University of California Santa Cruz) didn't help because thousands of these students snatched away anything affordable.

This made me a bit upset, that a local boy like me coming home from serving in the Army Rangers had a slim chance of finding a place to live.

We found a tiny downstairs studio for nine-hundred dollars a month. After we moved in, the upstairs was rented out to about five UCSC students. They were constantly having parties and bouncing a basketball off of the floor.

I was growing bitter toward UCSC and the whole new community that took control of my home town.

I got to surf a lot and that helped relieve some of the stress. But this was beginning to be stressful too because of the immense crowds filling every surf spot.

Never the less, I was really getting into the surf scene again. I remember surfing better than I ever had before. I was getting to know the new talent of young surfers in the lineup.

Jay Moriarity was one of the young surfers I got to know. He always asked me what it was like being in the Army Special Operations. He told me how his dad was in the Army and asked me a lot of questions about what it was like.

I told him that many of the guys in Special Operations were basically married to their unit. Their whole world was tied up in their group of men and they often chose them over their families.

He was a great guy and I loved surfing with him. Jay had this unique positive, joy filled attitude.

After a few years of surfing the overcrowded point breaks of Santa Cruz I was beginning to burn out. So I started getting into fishing for Steelhead in the San Lorenzo river.

Between the river and the ocean fishing, Santa Cruz surprisingly had a lot to offer. I guess it was in my blood, my dad fished that old river in the sixties and early seventies.

It is a pristine river in certain parts even to this day. The towering Redwood tree forest of the Gorge along Highway 9 was mysterious and magical. It was there that these mighty fish would swim powerfully upstream after spending two to four years out in the immense Pacific Ocean.

I was so into it. It was a great way to relax and get out into the fresh mountain air while fishing for the chrome sea running, rainbow trout.

One winter day I got up around four in the morning and it was still very dark out. I hiked down into the Gorge by moonlight and it was amazing. The moon rays were actually beaming down through the giant Redwood trees and I heard a pack of Coyotes howling. I hiked to one of the best Steelhead holes on the river called "Rincon Hole" and it was shimmering in the silvery moon light.

As soon as I cast into the shallow moving riffle water my line seemed to glide down at the perfect speed into the moon lit pool. Though I couldn't see anything I could feel the line tighten and rhythmically tap just like a Steelhead bites.

As soon as I whipped the eight-foot rod up, I knew a large Steelhead was hooked. It began to head shake with long sweeping motions and then the chrome sided fish flew into the air about five feet high. The silver sides reflected the moon light brighter than the glassy river surface. This fish was big as it was well above twelve pounds.

While fighting this fish the Coyotes started up again and I my adrenaline was kicking in full. The fish ended up shaking the hook out of its mouth and I lost the fish. This didn't bother me one bit that I had lost the fish because the whole experience was great. About ten minutes later light started to fill the Gorge and mist was rising off of the moving river. It was literally, "Gorgeous".

About a year later, in the fall I got up early to fish the lower stretches of the river that ran through the heart of

Santa Cruz. These areas sometimes held big fish that were coming in and out with the tides before the rains. I started out just downstream of the County building.

It was a clear, crisp November morning and as I trekked over the levy and down into the willow trees I immediately saw garbage spread out all over. In my mind I thought, "Those stinking city officials are ruining my city by allowing all of these homeless bums do this".

As I found a nice strip of gravel bar I made my way into the knee high riffle water. Ah, the sound of that rushing water always healed my soul.

As I worked my way, wading upstream, I wasn't getting any bites or seeing any signs of fish.

Then as the sun was peeking through the trees and starting to sparkle off of the riffle water I saw a silver reflection flash in front of me in the river. After casting toward it a few times with no bites, I walked closer and noticed it was a small dead Steelhead Trout of about a foot and a half long.

I waded up to it and looked at it. As I looked something caught my attention at about one hundred feet upstream. It was a guy washing his clothes in the river.

"That's it." I mumbled under my breath.

"That homeless scumbag killed this fish with his contaminated clothing," I thought this with bitterness and rage in my heart.

As I kept wading upstream I saw by his appearance this man wasn't like the other homeless I have seen. He was skinny, not the drug user skinny, but more like healthy in good shape kind of skinny.

Then I noticed he was motivated and organized in his movements. He was rolling up his bed roll which looked like a wool blanket. As I got closer he stopped, and walked straight toward me as if on a mission.

He walked right up to the edge of the river and stood on a clump of reeds mixed with gravel. It was like a natural podium for giving a speech.

I thought, "Please don't talk to me, I hate you."

As I was trying to wade past him he stopped me with power in his words by saying in a friendly voice, "How are you?"

I refused to answer but something inside me said, "Listen to him".

He said, "Fishing for trout today?"

"Yep", I responded.

"You know, Jesus said, 'Follow me and I will make you

fishers of men.'"

I stood there not knowing what to think or how to respond to what was just said. But something was beginning to burn inside of my heart to where I knew God had appointed this moment.

Then he began to speak to me as if an invisible Bible was opened right in front of him. The words came out pure and true. In the same way that the sunshine on a cold day can instantly warm your back, so too his words seemed to radiate through my skin and into my heart.

Then he said, "Make no mistake. It is not by your good works or how good of a person you are or think you are. This will not get you into the kingdom of paradise, which is the Kingdom of God. No. It is only by the work that Jesus did on the cross. It's only by God's mercy and grace that you will enter into his kingdom. It is by His Grace alone. It is a free gift of God which was bought for you at the cross."

After he said these words I could hardly even look at him. I felt like a kid who stole a chocolate candy bar and had it smeared all over his lips and hands. I was guilty of thinking I was good with God because I was a hardworking, good deed doing kind of a person. But I knew my attitude was bad before walking up to that homeless man. I knew I was hating on him before I ever even met him, or knew anything about his life.

So there I was being humbled as the sun was just starting to shine on me. The water was sparkling, the mist was rising up from the rushing water, the man of God stood there looking at me as I looked down in shame.

I looked upstream and gazed at the sparkling sun reflecting on the river and said, "You hit the nail right on the head".

He looked at me with a joy filled confident expression, turned around, picked up his bedroll and walked away.

Was that an angel sent from God?

Whatever he was doesn't matter. What matters is God spoke through him and right into my heart. I now saw my sin and was convicted of that sin.

It was like that song, "Amazing Grace". I knew that it was God's loving grace, "How sweet the sound that saved a wretched man like me". I realized I was not good at all, but a wretched sinner.

Afterward I fished my way a few miles upstream, reflecting on what the man said to me. It was near the old tannery that I finally found a decent steelhead fishing hole. The deep green depression in the middle of the river looked perfect.

I took a cast upstream and immediately my fishing line stopped bouncing down with the current, but the line danced in place. I instinctively tightened up my line and whipped the rod up to set the hook.

It felt as if I had snagged a log on near the bottom because there was no movement for a good five seconds.

Suddenly the line moved with lightning speed to the other side of the river as my reel was making a fast winding sound. The chrome and rainbow colored fish caused whitewater to explode up as it thrashed and then leaped high into the air.

After a long battle with this fish I was finally able to land it. It was a healthy, fresh out of the ocean, bright shining steelhead trout. It was about two feet long and weighed about five pounds.

I couldn't have been more stoked. A smile was stuck to face.

After I admired the fish for a few minutes I picked it up by the gill plate and began my hike downstream. After about a half a mile down I noticed a group of young homeless guys yelling as they ran down from the wood line out into the open gravel bar that lined the river.

They yelled, "Nice fish. Did you catch that in this river?"

I still felt the burning in my heart from the preaching to me earlier that morning and this time my attitude was sweet toward these homeless guys.

"You bet", I said with a smile and total respect for all four of these drug-addicted-looking guys.

They surrounded me just to see that beautiful fish and I was glad to show them. The awesome thing was that warm feeling in my heart grew and made me glad in my soul. I felt a renewed peace that day. It was as if God was shining his face upon me.

Later I stopped by my dad's place and showed him the fish. He was stoked because he loved steelhead fishing in the old days so it was refreshing to him to see one again so early in the season.

I shared the story of the man who preached the powerful grace message to me at the river's edge. That really refreshed my dad. He told me that he got goose bumps just listening to it. My dad was blessed by what God did that day and so was I.

The years passed by while living in Santa Cruz. I was

working full time with a heavy construction company and surfed much less than the previous years.

During this time, I had become friends with a great man named Chris. We ended up becoming best friends. He stood about six foot five and was solid muscle. He had the nickname, "Sasquatch" on the job site.

Working with him was always an adventure because he reminded me of those elite commandos that I used to work with. He was every bit as tough and fearless as any Delta Force operator. I saw him pick things up that most strong men couldn't budge and he was always willing to jump in the ditch and do any of the toughest jobs. He gained my respect right away and I was glad to have him as my leader.

We became close friends because of our work ethic and also because we had a lot in common. We both grew up surfing, fishing, and both of us were second generation Santa Cruz locals.

During our long drives to and from jobs we talked about everything. We talked about politics, our wives, surfing, fishing, how the University was destroying Santa Cruz, and much more. We also talked about Jesus.

Even though I was brought up in the Calvary Chapel type, "Jesus Movement" church, and he being Catholic, we both understood we needed Jesus for everything.

Chris was a follower of Jesus. He reminded me of that Disciple of Jesus named Peter because he was a fisherman, a fighter, and a born leader.

One weekend Chris asked me if I wanted to volunteer with him to help rebuild the Holy Cross Catholic school playground. I agreed and we worked most of the day on it. It felt good to do this work with him.

Later we received a big "Thank you Chris and George for your service, you are a couple of Angles" from the school Nuns. They wrote this up in the school newsletter for the whole school to see.

Chris showed me the newsletter and as I read it, a name jumped off of the pages at me. The "Thank you for your help" came from the teachers as well. Then I saw the name of a man who was my teacher when I was six years old. This was a different school which was in Santa Cruz back in the 1970's and it was there that he called me "Stupid" repeatedly in front of the whole class.

Immediately those horrid childhood emotions filled my chest. I felt this bitter pain in my heart which grew to hate. I realized I hated this man. I had never forgiven him for what he said to me and I even blamed him for a learning disability which plagued my psyche.

I was in shock by this. I soon started to realize that God had arranged this for me to get me healed. I started to ask God why it all happened and why I should forgive him.

I knew it had to be so. After the man at the river spoke God's word into my heart I knew I must forgive. I was able to forgive over time through much talking and pouring my heart out to God. This was the powerful work of God as I realized that it really was about the love, mercy and grace that came from Jesus as He was nailed to the cross. That teachers sin was nailed to that cross as well as my sins too.

This was a great miracle in my soul. Perhaps you need to forgive someone in your life too. I am here to tell you that it is a "must" for your own healing. You must forgive or relive it in your heart over and over again. The good news is that Jesus, the Son of God, can and will help you to release that person from your wrath. The Son will set you free, but you must set everyone else free who have wronged you as well.

The key to forgive is to realize God had his hand in all that has happened to you. Not just the good stuff but the tough stuff as well. We must realize his divine hand in all of it. When we see that, and yield to Him then we are free to receive His healing. It's like approaching a Roundabout; you must yield or it will harm you. You must yield to God and He will bring you through it.

Old testament Joseph was thrown into pit by his own brothers and later sold down the road as a slave. Then he was falsely accused of rape and thrown into prison. What we see in Joseph's story is that he never blamed God. He understood that God had his hand in all of it. He knew everything that happened to him was going to work for the good, for him and his family.

That is what happened years later. His brothers came back to beg for food and they didn't even know who Joseph was. Joseph was powerful and could have had them killed but instead he forgave them and blessed them as well as all of their families.

Joseph finally said to his brothers, "I am Joseph your brother". They were shocked by that and began feeling the weight of their sin, but Joseph said this to them, "Do not be grieved or angry with yourselves because you sold me here; for God sent me before you to preserve life…to save your lives by a great deliverance. So now it was not you who sent me here, but God."

Joseph showed mercy and grace to them who hurt him

years earlier. He showed that same loving kindness and tender mercies that Jesus showed to those who hurt him. This is the only way to be free and healed of all wrongs suffered in our lives. You must acknowledge God's hand in all of it.

People who have done great things in life have been hurt deeply first.

There was a boy who was told by his teacher that he was "Too stupid to learn anything". His name was, Thomas Edison the great inventor of the light bulb.

After being cut from his high school basketball team, he went home, locked himself in his room and cried. Who was he? Michael Jordan, the six time NBA champion.

He wasn't able to speak until he was almost four years old and his teachers said he would, "Never amount to much". His name was, Albert Einstein. He was a theoretical physicist and Nobel Prize winner.

Fired from a newspaper company for "Lacking imagination" and "Having no original ideas." Who was this? None other than Walt Disney, the creator of Mickey Mouse and winner of twenty-two Academy Awards.

The love of his life, whom he was engaged to be married to, died. He failed in business and he had a nervous breakdown. Later he was defeated in eight elections. This man was none other than the sixteenth President of the United States, Abraham Lincoln.

I know some of the children that I grew up with in that ministry community were hurt in deep and terrible ways but even they must forgive. If this speaks of you, release it to the God of the Universe who created you and knows everything about you. Jesus is Lord, and he loves you and wants you to come home to Him. He wants what is best for you, and He wants you and me to spend forever with Him in His kingdom of paradise.

Around 2004, while on the job in San Jose, my manager came running over to me and said, "George, your wife just called from Stanford Children's Hospital, there's something wrong with your son.

My heart immediately sank down deep, as if it fell to my feet. "My son? Lord please spare my son from anything bad", I prayed in my mind.

It took me about twenty minutes to get to Stanford Hospital. I was praying to God the whole time.

When I walked into the emergency room, I saw my wife and as soon as she saw me she began to weep while embracing me. At that very moment they were holding our little baby boy down so they could draw blood. His little body fought hard against the caring nurses, and eventually they were able to get the blood sample.

His whole body was a yellowish pale color and so the Doctors suspected he had cancer. When they told us that, my wife buried her head into my chest and cried out, "No". I was beginning to lose it as well but I was able to control myself and kept the flood of tears back.

Later that night, they set us up in a critical care room. We carefully watched the oxygen level monitor which was attached to the end of his finger. Sometimes it would alarm and the nurses would rush in but somehow it would go right back up to one hundred percent oxygen.

He was so lethargic and pale. It was so heart breaking.

Our little Douglas was dying. This was a hopeless feeling and all we could do was pray and that we did constantly. We prayed continuously and a certain peace came over our room. We knew we were not alone because we both felt the presence of God with us.

The Doctor told us that his red blood cells were nearly gone because his own antibodies were attacking his red blood cells and platelets. He told us his platelet count was dangerously low. But he stopped and told us it was a miracle that his oxygen level was one hundred percent. Then he said, "We can't explain it, but we see strange miracles like this with children."

The next day a team of Doctors came in and examined him while brainstorming what he had. They told us they weren't sure what was wrong but assured us they were researching everything possible.

Finally, after all day they came back and the lead Doctor said they determined he had a rare syndrome called, "Evan's Syndrome". He then told us that the only chance he had was to find a perfect blood match to fight this through a blood transfusion. But he told me that it was no guarantee and that we needed to be prepared for the worst.

After what seemed like a thousand years they came to us and said they had found a good blood match. Immediately my wife and I praised and thanked God.

When the nurse came in with the blood my instincts kicked in and I became very protective of that blood. This blood was precious and priceless to us. This blood was going to give my dying son life.

As she positioned the blood in the intravenous holder I stood there with my hands cupped underneath just in case she dropped it. She pushed the soft clear tube into the blood bag and connected the other end of the tube into our baby's arm.

She opened the little valve and I watched carefully as the precious blood flowed down and into his almost lifeless body. As it flowed into our baby boy, he began to come to life.

Christina and I now had tears of joy as we watched the yellow pale cheeks turn rosy red immediately. We literally saw new life in him. He began to giggle and roll around with a big smile. He actually rolled over for the first time right there in that room.

We saw him saved by this new blood which healed him of his disease. While I witnessed all of this I found a profound purpose to what we experienced. I knew God had shown me how precious his Son's blood was to Him.

The Father watched his only Son give his precious life giving blood to all of us who suffer the disease of sin. It was the opposite of what my wife and I saw. God the Father watched the precious blood flow out of his Son and He died to save us. I watched that precious blood flow in and my son's life was saved and restored to life.

About two years later I was on a construction project building a bridge south of Santa Cruz. This was a tough job with my best friend Chris as he was the Foreman.

He was a great foreman and friend. We spent a lot of time Salmon fishing, Abalone diving, and surfing together.

Chris was and still is my best friend.

One week, near the end of the bridge job, Chris was sent to a new job in Carmel. While working, my manager came up to me and said, "Chris was in a bad accident. The excavator he was operating flipped over and he was pinned under it. They just medevacked him by helicopter to Stanford Hospital.

My heart sank deep again just like it did with my son. "No Lord", I said to myself. I knew this was very serious. So I dropped everything and jumped into my truck and rushed to Stanford hospital.

On the way to the Hospital I prayed, wept, and prayed more for my best friend. "Lord don't let him die", I prayed fervently while driving over the Santa Cruz mountains.

I arrived at the hospital at exactly the same time as his wife Gina and daughter. I told her, "I am so sorry about what happened and that I would continue to pray for Chris". We got into the elevator together and I didn't know what to do for them but to just be there for them.

I was able to get them water and some food. At that point the CEO of the company showed up and told us that his friend was working on Chris in the emergency room and that he was in good hands.

After Chris was sent to Emergency surgery I drove home, took a shower and tried to go to sleep. It was about midnight when I went to bed. I tossed and turned in bed. Sleep was far from me as I knew my best buddy was in a battle for his life.

I looked at the time and it read "3:00 am".

At that very moment a peace fell over me. I suddenly felt at ease and a certain warmness in my heart. It was like a little boy trying to sleep during a lightning storm, scared stiff when suddenly his dad puts his strong hand gently on his shoulder and says, "It's going to be alright buddy, I am here now and I will stay here."

I had a sudden peace, settled deep into my bed slept good and sound. I even woke up feeling good and peaceful about my friend's wellbeing.

He survived the surgery and I thanked God. During his recovery time my wife and I were packing up our stuff to move up to the Pacific Northwest. We had already planned on moving to Washington state over the past few months but I was sad to leave my best friend, especially in the condition he was in.

I was able to visit him a couple of times. One time he was totally out, as he must have been medicated. I left him one of my favorite water color paintings of the Santa Cruz Harbor. I got to visit him just before our move and this time he was in much better shape. Gina was there and so was the owner of our construction company.

He talked about the surgery and we joked a bit. He told us how he was able to lift the Excavator Tractor up even though it weighed thousands of pounds. He said he thought of his wife and daughters as the monstrous machine had him pinned down.

He jokingly told us that the medics put him in the helicopter and one of them shut the sliding door on his foot. Chris said he let out a loud scream and the medics eyes bulged out in fear. We all laughed.

After about an hour his family was getting hungry and they left for the cafeteria to have lunch. I stayed with Chris and as soon as they left the room, Chris said, "George I have something I have to tell you".

He said, "While I was being operated on in the ER, I

went into severe traumatic shock. When this happened I was gone, my heart stopped and I remember being in this most beautiful place. There was a meadow with bright flowers with a small rock wall and I knew it was heaven. Everything in me wanted to walk right over that wall because of how good it was. But as I was about to step over I knew Jesus was there and he said to me, 'You can come over, but if you do there is no going back'. I immediately thought of my girls and at that moment I awoke to the bright light of the operating table as the Doctors were yelling 'Stay with us Chris'. My body was convulsing violently but I knew I was going to see my girls again."

He said to me, "This happened at three in the morning".

I couldn't believe what I heard. So I told him how I couldn't sleep that night and then the peace I experienced right at three in the morning.

Chris was so happy about Jesus. He told me how beautiful it was at the very Gates of Heaven and how indescribably good that place was.

I drove home that day with a renewed faith in Jesus. I knew he loved Chris and his family. I knew he doesn't care if your Catholic, Protestant, Jewish, Evangelical, or even a "Nothing". It's a personal thing with him. It's not about your religious title or group. It is about believing in Jesus as your Lord and Savior. Its about wanting to know him and being with him.

God gives everyone exactly what they want ultimately. If you want nothing to do with God, then he will grant your wish. On the other hand, if you want to be with Him then you will love and want to be with His Son, Jesus.

So, to go to hell is getting what you really want. Hell is total separation from God. It is the outer darkness far away from His presence, because God is light, and His son Jesus is the "Light of the world".

To go to heaven is to get what you want. It's to be with Jesus forever. Just as an engaged bride wants to be with her groom. It is an open invitation to be in the light and Jesus is the light. He is the Way. He is the only way to heaven.

The Same Today

Chapter Six: The Return

It was time for us to get out of Santa Cruz.

My wife, our toddler son and I ended up moving to Vancouver, Washington.

We enjoyed the Portland Zoo, the Columbia Gorge waterfalls and the Oregon coast. I loved fishing the Kalama river for Steelhead and caught a few nice fish. But this was not the place for us and we knew it.

We ended up taking a weekend trip up north to Sequim and Port Angeles, Washington. The moment we rounded the last corner and drove into Sequim, my wife and I had a peace, a certain peace about this place.

This is ironic because about a year earlier, while living in Santa Cruz, I was looking at a map of Washington state and I put my finger on this place and told Christina that this is where we need to move.

So fast forward over a year and we were driving through that exact same spot feeling God's peace and knowing it was meant to be. We went to the beaches, looked at the rivers, drove through Sequim and we loved it.

We looked at each other and knew this was the place. The same day we linked up with a real estate lady who showed us around. The real estate boom was in full force at this time and we found nothing that whole day. Then she took us into a community of houses in our price range just hoping we would find something before investors out bid us with cash offers.

We found a house that was for sale, just listed that morning. It was almost new, two bedroom, two bath, beautiful house in a sweet location.

The moment we walked into the house we felt the peace of God resting on us. We walked in with our little Douglas smiling and running in like it was is his house. The owner looked over at us and smiled.

Standing next to the owner were two men from the city of Seattle who were offering him far more than the price he was originally asking. He ignored the two men, introduced himself to us with a warm hand shake, and said, "Hi, my name is Bob".

Bob had a sweet spirit about him and he just made us feel good to talk to him. He asked us about our situation and how old our son was. He showed us around the house as a knowledgeable builder. He then told us he had built it for him and his wife and that she had passed away about a year earlier.

Then he said to us, "I want you guys to live in this house and so I am going to give it to you for the asking price".

My wife and I were in utter shock at what he just said. We were elated, just filled with joy and relief.

We headed back to the real estate office and met Bob and his wife there.

As we talked with our agent we found out she was a believer in Jesus and Bob and his wife as well. So then Bob asked if we could all pray together before starting the whole process. We prayed together and it was sweet.

The next morning, I woke up in our motel room in Port Angeles and realized we had just bought a house.

After thanking God for guiding us to that perfect house for us, I knew I needed to get off of my butt, and look for a job. So, I gave my wife and boy a kiss and asked her to pray for me as I went out to look for a job.

So I was driving down the main street of Port Angeles heading east, I realized this was critical to find a job and it was a bit frightening. But even though the circumstances were piled high against finding a good job I knew deep down that God was making a way.

Driving past the Post Office on the right, I thought, "Ok Lord where should I go? Is it the Post Office?"

I knew it wasn't the Post Office.

Then just a couple of miles east on the other side of the road I saw a building that had a sign out in front, "PUD". I had no idea what the sign meant nor did I know anything else about this place but something inside me said, "Turn around and go there".

I walked in and there were a few friendly customer service representatives there ready to help. So I asked, "Do you have any job openings?"

The courteous lady said, "As a matter of fact, we do".

She gave me a sheet of paper that had the job description which seemed tailor-made for me because they asked for experience in construction of water lines and pump stations. The position was in the Water Department for this public utility company. That's what the "PUD" stood for Public Utility District.

Under the title was the starting pay rate of twenty-three dollars an hour. I immediately knew that God had guided me there. So I drove straight back to tell my wife and showed her the job announcement sheet. We were so stoked.

A few weeks later they called me in for an interview. It was a rare seventy degrees, a sunny day in March and the interview felt good. It just seemed like I was going to get the job.

A few days later my wife and I were in our rented apartment in Vancouver and the phone rang. It was the PUD. The lady told me she was glad to offer me the job in the water department. I was so happy. Everything just seemed to fall into place for us.

That same night my wife turned the TV on and I heard the music start, "God sent His son, they called him Jesus". It was a song we used to sing a lot in the 70's during the Jesus movement titled, "Because He Lives, I Can Face Tomorrow".

I found my heart feeling warm as if I was on my way home. I knew God was showing me that He was in control, that He's the same today, and I could trust Him for tomorrow and forever.

This was shortly after the September 11th, 2001 terror attack on our country. So there was a certain fear in our country, "When is the next attack"? So when I heard these four men sing this song there was power in it. It was filled with the power of the Lord, as they sang, "Because He lives, I can face tomorrow."

It also spoke into my heart because only days before I feared that I wouldn't find a job up in our new home town. It was a sense of, "My Father God has it all in his hands and just look at how He takes care of His children."

After a year of working with the PUD they hired me on full time. I had to be a meter reader for a year before going back to the Water Department full time.

The years went by and my wife was now pregnant with our second son. At this point I was working full time in the Water Department.

I fit in with the crew pretty well. I never showed anyone that I was a Christian at first. I was too worried about what they would think of me. I heard jokes about Christians and a general dislike for them, but I never spoke up about it.

Then one day I was driving around the beautiful Lake Crescent, listening to the Christian radio station. The song came on, "It's all about you Jesus". And when the part of the song came on, "Jesus, lover of my soul", I started to feel something in my heart. I knew I was ashamed of Him at work, yet He still loved my soul. I wept bitterly on that road. I felt the same shame that Peter must have felt when he denied Jesus three times.

This was the catalyst for my return home to the Lord.

Later that year my dad invited me to go with him to, "Northwest Men's Conference". It was held at the Calvary Fellowship in Mount Lake Terrace. The founding pastor is a man named Wayne Taylor, who is an awesome teacher and follower of Jesus.

Wayne was one of the original guys who were taught by Chuck Smith in the early Calvary Chapel days. He was there with my first pastor, Skip Heitzig. He was also there with Greg Laurie, and Jon Courson and these two men were the main speakers at this conference.

When Greg Laurie spoke, he taught through the prodigal son story in Luke chapter fifteen. I was moved in my heart as the story unfolded. It was about a son who wanted freedom from his father and left him to go party. After some time that son realized he was way better off with his father than with party crowd.

As Greg taught, my heart was breaking and I knew God the Father was speaking into my heart through his story. You see, his lost son just starts to turn back to his father and the father immediately started blessing him. That was like my experience around the lake and all the other times he saved me and helped me by His mercy and grace.

At the end of the teaching, Greg prayed and asked if there were any men who knew they were a "Prodigal" son who needs to come home to the Father. As he said those words, I knew in my heart it was me. There was no denying it and so I dearly wanted to be fully restored to my God.

He said, "If this is you, stand up right where you are and pray a prayer to re-commit to Jesus". As I stood I looked around and noticed I was the only one standing among over one thousand men. I was thinking, "Come on Lord, just me?" But I was going through with it anyway. At that point a few other men rose to their feet.

After I prayed that prayer from my heart, and with my lips, I felt an immediate relief, and a warm burning love in my heart. I knew it was for real and deep into my soul. I got home and was so excited to tell my wife. She was surprised by all of it.

Now I was renewed and following Jesus. I was not

perfect but I was renewed. The next Monday at work I made a stand for Jesus. Some of the guys were talking about how much of a hypocrite this Christian man was that they had worked with years ago.

I told them that we are all hypocrites at times. I said, "I am a Christian and I can tell you that I will probably wrong you and be a hypocrite about it at one time or another, but it's about who I know, not how good I am".

There was a new kind of silence after I said this. Suddenly, I was no longer one of the guys, so to speak. I started to get the cold shoulder from my leader and a few of the others in the department.

I kept remembering Biblical Joseph and how his brothers hated him. That story kept playing over and over in my heart and mind. It was a tough time but God helped me.

One day a card was handed over to me in the morning tailboard meeting. The card had a picture of a bunch of dogs peeing on a fire hydrant that was trying to disguise itself as a dog. The words said, "We know you're not one of us". I opened the card and inside it was signed by everyone on the crew. I felt horrible but I knew it was persecution because I now shined with Jesus' light as a follower of Him.

I kept remembering Joseph and how he was close to God, but was hated by many. Then I thought of how Jesus was hated by His own. He was hated and He was God, sent from heaven to rescue the world. So I knew I would be rejected too and deep down it was okay.

This helped me understand, as I read the Bible - which is the word of God – I started to see that Joseph was a living picture story of Jesus Himself. He was a reflection of Jesus before Jesus was born as a man.

After all, both were the father's most favored son; both were hated by their own brethren; both were sold for silver; both handed over to the Gentiles; they were both falsely accused; they were both condemned; while being condemned they both tell the fate of the two with them, one is restored, the other is cursed; they were both raised up out of the place of the condemned; they were both exalted to the right hand of the throne; they were both given Gentile brides (The Church); both were to be the Savior in a future time of world trouble; both save their brethren who were the whole house of Israel, during the time of great trouble; both bring their whole family together at the end – their Gentile brides and their brethren the sons of Israel.

This story of Joseph in the book of Genesis gave me insight into how to interpret other parts of the Bible such as: Revelation, Daniel, and Ezekiel.

God had a plan with Joseph, and I believe he weaved in his future plan. Interesting isn't it? The best commentary for explaining the Bible is the Bible itself. Joseph's story showed just that.

I shared this with my friend one morning as we were driving out to go surfing. He asked me to prepare a teaching on it for his church which was a Calvary Chapel.

I was given two Wednesday nights to teach on this "Joseph like Jesus" teaching. I was a bit scared to teach but once I started God helped me greatly. Many were blessed by the teaching.

I just kept studying the Bible and writing down more and more into the notes of the teaching. Then I discovered that I should turn these notes into a book.

Later that year, my friends and I were at the Northwest Pastors and Leaders conference, at the same Calvary Fellowship where I renewed my walk with the Lord. At this conference, Jon Courson's son Ben gave a powerful message. In it he declared, "Go on that mission's trip, write that book for the Lord". When he said that I realized I should write and I did.

I ended up writing "Joseph" and later, from another teaching "Road to Emmaus". The word of God is shown in both books and the good news of God's grace is preached in each book. My hope is for the good news of Jesus shines brightly in all of these books that I have written.

The Same Today

Chapter Seven: The Same Today

God still does those same miracles today that he did around the time of Jesus, because He's the same today.

I worked with an eighty plus year old man named Fritz. He was the most loving, caring, selfless man I had ever met. He was all about Jesus, then others and it showed in his life.

He knew we were new in town and that my wife and I didn't know anyone in the area and so he made sure to be there for us.

He was an amazing old man. He worked harder than most of the young guys. He would jump into the ditch and take the shovel from you to give you a break.

My family and I started going to church with Fritz and his lovely wife. Fritz kept mini candy bars in his jacket pockets for all of the little kids. They would run to him as soon as church ended and he was like Santa Clause to those kids. Hey called all of the boys, "Buckshot". "Here you go buckshot", he would say to them as he handed them the candy.

Fritz and his wife often would take us out to breakfast or lunch after church. We became such good friends and we felt like we were a part of their family.

The name of the church is called, "Independent Bible Church." It was and still is a great church, full of people who love God. We enjoyed the times we went even though it was a long drive from Sequim.

One Sunday my parents came up to visit from Santa Cruz and they were happy to go to church with us. I really wanted my parents to meet Fritz. We were a bit late but sure enough we looked over the large crowd and found Fritz. Somehow there was plenty of room for our family to sit next to them.

During the greeting time I introduced my parents to Fritz. He told my dad that I was one of the best workers he ever worked with. I knew that wasn't really true but he was such a kind man, and he was always bragging about others.

Something caught my attention on this day when I

looked at Fritz. His skin looked extremely pale and he even had a yellowish color to his eyes and face. My wife even nudged me and asked me, "Is Fritz alright?"

The message was great. We sat as the pastor was finishing up his message with the usual closing song starting, "How Great is our God".

As we sat there feeling the peace and goodness of God I looked over at Fritz and his eyes were rolled way back. All I could see was mostly the white and yellowish part as the pupils were turned up and inward.

My first thought was, "He's dead". He looked dead to me.

While the beautiful song was being sung I said, "Fritz, are you alright." There was no response.

His wife looked over at him and yelled, "Fritz. No. No Fritz."

She took off, running up the isle and out the doors.

I told the guy sitting behind us to call 911.

At this point the whole row was starting to notice. The kind lady in front of Fritz turned around and started supporting his head with her hands. As she did this she told me she was a nurse.

I didn't see him breathing and I was starting to worry.

I asked God, "Lord please help him and what should I do"?

At that moment I could hear the words "Touch his hand."

Not one to argue in moments like that I was obedient to what I knew I had to do and held his lifeless cold hand.

As soon as I held his hand something amazing happened. It warmed up instantly and he squeezed my hand. Then his eyes came back to normal and his skin looked good.

He turned his head and looked right into my eyes like he would any other day and said, "Hey buckshot". He then reached into his jacket pocket and grabbed a king size snickers candy bar and offered it to me.

I was blown away at what God had just done. All I did was obey his prompting and he restored my friend instantly. That song the church was singing, "How Great is our God" was perfect for that moment.

Meanwhile, his wife came back down the aisle with the Paramedics following her. One of the medics loudly said, "Fritz". My old friend turned around and yelled, "What do you want? And why are you here?"

They said to him, "We need to get you into this stretcher

and take you to the hospital".

Fritz said, "I'm not going anywhere with you guys. I am just fine."

His wife shouted, "Just go with them Fritz".

And with that he got up and sat down on their wheeled stretcher.

As I am writing this down, that sweet old man is still alive. This happened about seven years ago. God is good and he still does the same miracles today.

One Monday morning I heard a co-worker who worked in the materials department - singing the song, "When the Role is Called up Yonder I'll be There".

He looked at me with a smile and said, "How about you George, will you be there". I answered, "Yes". But inside I was asking myself, "Will I be there?"

As I drove my company truck I felt so condemned, so accused, so guilty. I started to ask God, "Am I really one of yours?"

I wasn't feeling like I was a good Christian because just weeks earlier I had a couple of outbursts of anger. The outbursts just kept playing over and over again in my mind as I drove for twenty minutes.

Then, I turned on a road that went toward the towering, majestic, Olympic Mountains. As I drove it was overcast and grey with no view of the beautiful snowcapped mountains.

Then as I was still wrestling with whether or not I was a legitimate child of God, the clouds parted and the sun shown on the freshly snow covered ridgeline. Mist was billowing up through the bright white ridgeline.

I turned the radio on and just as soon as I turned it on the song just started, "When the trumpet of the Lord shall sound, and time will be no more, and the morning breaks eternal bright and fair, when the saved of earth shall gather, over on the other shore, and the roll is called up yonder, I'll be there!"

As soon as I heard the song start I felt the presence of my good Lord, it was as if he was sitting in the truck with me and put his hand on my shoulder. My heart just melted within me and my eyes welled up with tears of joy. I pulled over and just soaked in the rest of that old hymn.

Then my God just spoke into my heart, "My son don't worry, you are one of mine, and yes, when that roll is called up yonder you will be there".

This experience was nothing short of a miracle. Not a miracle like "Signs and wonders", but a miracle of love and assurance that I belonged to Jesus. I had listened to that radio station every day and I never heard that song played until that very moment when I turned it on. God is so good.

Yes, I had been saved and born again at the age of thirteen, and yes I had rededicated my life to the Lord seven years before this moment at the Men's Conference, but I felt like I was no good. I knew I was a failure and that I was not worthy to go to heaven. What I didn't realize fully was that when God looks at me He is not looking at me alone with all of my failures. He is looking at me marked by the blood of His Son Jesus. He is seeing the seal, the flame of the Holy Spirit in me, however dim the flame is in me, it is still His flame.

About a year after this experience I was in a Christian group that met once a month. We would read books and then meet up and talk about them.

We read many good books that encouraged me to serve Jesus. We read "The Great Divorce" by C.S. Lewis, "Living Water" by Chuck Smith, and many other excellent books.

Then we read a modern Christian book that emphasized that you may not be a real follower of Jesus if you're not doing enough for Jesus. The book seemed great at first until this sickening feeling came over me that made me doubt that I was even a legitimate child of God.

The whole concept of the book was not to be a mere fan of God. That you must be a close follower of God or you are an illegitimate child of God.

It all sounded right to me until one of my buddies who was in our group came to me and said, "Have you been reading that book?"

I said, "Yes, how about you?"

"I have and now I don't feel like I am really even a Christian," he told me with a look of discouragement.

I knew this guy was a believer and a follower of Jesus and this had me concerned.

I told him to be careful of that teaching because the book was making me feel the same way, and I know, that I know I am one of God's children.

I became angry at the book. The reason for this is because I believe Satan himself loves to go around making Christians fell like they are illegitimate children of God. He loves to discourage God's people by putting doubt in their minds.

This is what makes believing in Jesus so different from all of the religions of the world. Most religions teach that you must do the work to reach heaven. Many legalistic Christian's believe it's by their good works and pure living. The Buddhists strive for nirvana, and Buddha himself said he never reached it. The Muslims work so hard to please Allah, and even believe in murdering the innocent to get to paradise.

No religion can give you grace. None of the religions of the world can promise life forever. But God can.

There is a God in Heaven who gives and forwards this gift of life directly to you through his son Jesus.

He forwards and gives. He for-gives. He "Forgives".

Gives what? You might ask.

Mercy and grace.

Mercy is not getting the justice that you and I deserve.

Grace is getting something good that we don't deserve.

It's that simple.

This forwarded gift is received like a package delivered to the door of our home. We only receive it when we open the door, and let Jesus in.

Jesus said, "I am the Way, the Truth, and the Life, and no one goes to the Father except by me."

He is The Way.

It's that simple.

An amazing miracle happened when my wife was pregnant with our second son.

I came home one day and she hugged me and started crying. She told me that the ultrasound had revealed a deformity in our baby. The local doctors told her that he was deformed and may even have a brain deformity. So they made an immediate appointment for us in Seattle.

We had the most state of the art technology used to look inside her womb. We were told to wait for a few hours as the Doctors analyzed the imagery, so we walked down the street to a nearby restaurant for breakfast.

As we sat there sipping coffee my wife broke down again. She was so emotional. The tears welled up and spilled out of her beautiful brown eyes. At that moment I heard the clearest words, "Don't worry, your son will be healthy and whole."

I immediately repeated it to my wife as she cried.

After breakfast we headed back up to the doctors. They had us wait in a room designed to show the advanced ultrasound imagery of her womb. The Doctor came in and showed us the pictures. She said, "The bad news is your baby has a deformed and short femur bone in his right leg. But the good news is, your baby is healthy and whole."

I was warmed up in my heart after hearing those same words again.

We immediately thanked God for the health of our baby.

Then the doctor gave us a disclaimer saying, "I am required to say this." She then told us that we had the option of "Terminating the Pregnancy".

We both immediately said, "No way".

She quickly said, "I agree with you two completely".

So our little boy, Louis, was born healthy and whole.

We had many routine appointments to Children's Hospital in Seattle. They took many x-rays and our Doctor was one of the best in the world at leg lengthening. He was a friendly guy who said he had helped hundreds of children with the exact same femur deformity that our son had.

He told us that what he had is exactly the same in every

other kid who has it. The right femur bone in the thigh, is shorter and twisted. The hip socket is shallow to nonexistent and will have to be rebuilt first.

We had numerous x-rays that showed the missing hip socket by the time Louis was two to three years old.

Well, the time came for the pre-surgery appointment for the hip socket construction. We were in the waiting room just before the last x-ray before surgery. My wife asked me to pray. We both laid our hands on his little hip and I remember praying a sincere heart felt prayer to our Lord. As I prayed I just knew that something had happened.

On our previous visits we told the Doctor that we were going to be praying for healing for our little boy. He responded with a skeptical, "Oh, yes faith can help". I said, "Not just faith, but faith in Jesus". This seemed to throw him off a bit as he was sarcastic about this.

So we prayed. We also had many of our friends and family praying. We also took him to the church where I recommitted my life to the Lord, and had Pastor Wayne and the elders pray for him.

After we prayed in that room, the x-ray person came in and took him. On a previous visit he said Louis was the strongest baby he had ever tried to hold down for an x-ray.

Our boy truly was exceptionally strong. We found him onetime upside down like a Koala Bear hanging on the vertical bars of his crib.

So they miraculously got the x-ray without a battle and returned him to our room. After a long wait, The Doctor came in with his young intern and brought up the images on the computer screen. He was looking at the x-ray and said, "There may be something wrong with the x-ray, or your son has a perfectly good hip socket."

The young doctor took a look as well and agreed that the hip socket was now there. He started comparing the previous images and scratched his head saying, "I can't explain this, I have never seen this. It's a freebee, he will not need the surgery. Let's go ahead and cancel it."

I smiled at him and said, "That prayer worked, because it was Jesus who healed him."

As I said that, the intern doctor was standing behind him smiling giving me a thumbs up. Then The Doctor left the room and the young intern stayed with us. He smiled at us and said, "Praise the Lord. Good job you guys. I am a believer as well. The Doctor needed to hear that."

Around this same time my older son Douglas told us one night that he had a strange lump on his collar bone. My wife and I looked at it and rand our fingers over it. It was about the size of a large grape and made us very concerned.

We made an appointment with the local pediatric hospital and they too were concerned. So they had us go to Children's Hospital in Seattle for expert analyses. This worked out great for us because Louis needed to go as well and we were able to schedule both of our boy's appointments in one trip.

At the appointment the Doctor examined the images and told us that it was in fact a tumor, but at this point it was not a threat. Never the less, he said that he wanted to watch it closely and have it removed.

Then the other Doctor came in to check on Louis leg and he was still amazed by Louis' hip. Then my wife showed him our older son's tumor on his collar bone. So they scheduled us to come again in six months and have both boy's appointments at the same time.

A few weeks later our family was sitting in the living room and our older son Douglas was laying on the couch reading his book. He spoke up in a casual way, "Oh hey mom and dad I forgot to tell you, that lump is gone.

I remember we prayed the night before for Jesus to heal him. We both ran our fingers over his collar bone and it was smooth.

So my wife and I just thanked God for this.

When we got to our appointment in Seattle we showed the doctor and he was amazed. He took x-rays anyway and showed them to us and he pointed out that it was all gone. He said they see these kinds of things happen with kids.

We stayed in that same room for Louis hip and leg appointment and his Doctor came in and examined our little one. After checking Louis, he looked over at Douglas who was busy playing his game on his tablet devise. He asked, "How is that tumor on his collar bone?"

We were glad to tell him that it was gone, completely gone. We told him Jesus healed him. The Doctor looked at us with a puzzled look and asked if he could take a look. So Douglas got up, pulled his tee shirt down and showed him the perfectly shaped collar bone.

As he looked he was amazed and ran his fingers across his collar bone over and over. I remember just smiling and thanking Jesus once again.

We have seen some amazing miracles in this book so far. I testify that every one of them is true. My wife can testify to the legitimacy of the later miracles as well.

Many people look at the miracles in the Bible and think, "God doesn't do miracles like that anymore". But God is "The Same Today". He's the same today, just as he was yesterday, and will be forever.

Many say, "The church is dead today compared to the church described in the book of Acts".

The book of Acts showed the miracles of the early church just after Jesus was resurrected. What many people miss is that these "Acts" took place over about a thirty-year span. So it shows us that these miracles happened over a long time. They could have gone for many years without one miracle.

This thirty year period was nothing like the three-and-a-half years during Jesus' ministry.

There was never a time of so many powerful miracles in such a short span of time as with Jesus. This is another amazing and special attribute of Jesus. This shows us He was not just man but that He was fully God and fully man in one.

But, was it all about the miracles?

No.

The physical miracles were part of His plan but He emphasized a much greater miracle than that.

The greatest miracles in life are not the healing miracles. They are not the miracles of angels helping us. Nor are they miracles of driving demons out or away. They certainly are not miracles of prophesying.

So what is the greatest miracle of all?

Are you ready for this?

Wait for it. Wait for it.

Yes, it is in God's word.

Now are you ready for it?

Yes, it is supernatural.

Here it is.

God's love.

It was His great love for you and me that nailed His Son to the cross. God paid for us with His greatest treasure of all, His only Son, Jesus. Through this, the greatest payment in history we are able to fully have His love in our hearts through relationship with Him.

It is His mighty love, planted and watered in our hearts that becomes the greatest miracle of all.

I am not talking about a human love. It's not, "Love that wins", but it's "God's greater love that wins."

We see this kind of love in the book of 1st Corinthians chapter thirteen in the Bible.

Let's take a look:

"Though I speak with the tongues of men and of angels, but have not love, I have become sounding brass or a clanging cymbal. And though I have the gift of prophecy, and understand all mysteries and all knowledge, and though I have all faith, so that I could remove mountains, but have not love, I am nothing. And though I bestow all my goods to feed the poor, and though I give my body to be burned, but have not love, it profits me nothing.

Love suffers long and is kind; love does not envy; love does not parade itself, is not puffed up; does not behave rudely, does not seek its own, is not provoked, thinks no evil; does not rejoice in iniquity, but rejoices in the truth; bears all things, believes all things, hopes all things, endures all things.

Love never fails. But whether there are prophecies, they will fail; whether there are tongues, they will cease; whether there is knowledge, it will vanish away. For we know in part and we prophesy in part. But when that which is perfect has come, then that which is in part will be done away.

When I was a child, I spoke as a child, I understood as a child, I thought as a child; but when I became a man, I put away childish things. For now we see in a mirror, dimly, but then face to face. Now I know in part, but then I shall know just as I also am known.

And now abide faith, hope, love, these three; but the greatest of these is love."

What an amazing treasure of scripture that chapter holds. These words reflect Jesus Christ directly. None of us are capable of that kind of love without Him giving it to us.

It is written in 1st John, in the Bible, which is the inspired words of God Himself, that "God is love".

Jesus was quoted as saying, "I and My Father are one".

So Jesus is God and God is Love.

Jesus Christ is Love.

He is that love that we saw in 1st Corinthians, chapter thirteen.

So you could read that chapter and use the name "Jesus" instead of "love". Or you could plug it in as, "Jesus' love" instead of "love".

Let's try it out:

Though I speak with the tongues of men and of angels, but have not **Jesus**, I have become sounding brass or a clanging cymbal. And though I have the gift of prophecy, and understand all mysteries and all knowledge, and though I have all faith, so that I could remove mountains, but have not **Jesus' love**, I am nothing. And though I bestow all my goods to feed the poor, and though I give my body to be burned, but have not **Jesus' love**, it profits me nothing.

Jesus suffers long and is kind; **His love** does not envy; **Jesus' love** does not parade itself, is not puffed up; does not behave rudely, does not seek its own, is not provoked, thinks no evil; does not rejoice in iniquity, but rejoices in the truth; bears all things, believes all things, hopes all things, endures all things.

Jesus' love never fails. But whether there are prophecies, they will fail; whether there are tongues, they will cease; whether there is knowledge, it will vanish away…And now abide faith, hope, **Jesus' love**, these three; but the greatest of these is **Jesus' love**.

The greatest miracle of all, is Jesus. He is love, and his love is great.

It is no wonder that John, who was the closest disciple of Jesus, said this, "Children (of God) love one another".

It is recorded by the church historians that when John was very old people would travel great distances to see and hear the last remaining disciple who walked closely with Jesus. They came to hear him preach a great message and some were disappointed. This is because John would sit there on a Sunday morning and the great crowds were in anticipation of his words but John would begin the message and end it with, "Little children, love one another."

"That's it? That's all you've got?" They would ask.

You see, John knew how important this simple message was.

So in his last years of life, history tell us, he would give this five-word sermon, "Little children love one another".

It got tedious, people were expecting a long sermon and so they complained. Tradition says one man came to him and said, "Brother John, might you not bring us something deeper?"

John replied, "Jesus gave us that command, and it doesn't get any deeper."

My wife and I have to live this love out every day.

She is very Catholic.

I am very Evangelical.

She believes in Jesus and she is one of His.

I believe in Jesus and am one of His.

We differ on many things such as: church history, styles of worship, eschatology, and much more.

Though we differ on these many things we both understand that we are saved by the work Jesus did on the cross.

We both believe that Jesus was born of the virgin Mary, conceived by the Holy Spirit, was fully man and fully God. He suffered and died on the cross for our sins and the sins of the world, was buried for three days, but on the third day was raised from the dead to life. We both believe He is seated at the right hand of the Father, and will come again for us in the future.

If we are truly His and have been "Born Again" by the Holy Spirit, then we will have **Jesus' love** in our hearts. This will be evident by our love for each other. Yes we make mistakes, we have our failures but overall His love is evident.

Remember Jesus said: "A good tree produces good fruit, and a bad tree produces bad fruit. A good tree can't produce bad fruit, and a bad tree can't produce good fruit.

So every tree that does not produce good fruit is chopped down and thrown into the fire. Yes, just as you can identify a tree by its fruit, so you can identify people by their actions."

The tree doesn't work on its own to produce the good fruit. It comes supernaturally without trying. God, who is the Great Gardener, waters the tree, feeds the tree all of the nutrients, and prunes the tree. The tree is just patiently waiting for the master gardener to take care of it.

When the tree blossoms it is beautiful. When it produces ripe, sweet, nutritious fruit it is good. All of this reflects the work of the Master Gardener who gave his work of loving kindness, not because of the work of the tree itself. Remember it's His grace.

I am commanded to love my wife as Christ loves his church. This means I give her the grace of loving kindness even when she does not deserve it.

I was not saved by my works. I did not earn my way to God. So why would I expect my wife to earn her way by being perfect.

"For by grace you have been saved through faith, and that not of yourselves; it is the gift of God, not of works, lest anyone should boast." (Ephesians 2:8-9)

Every day we struggle in our differences but our God is the same. He never changes. He is the same God as He was from the very beginning of our world. He will be the same God in the future.

Hebrews chapter thirteen says, "Jesus Christ is the same yesterday, today, and forever."

This gives us great hope.

He is the same today.

If you don't know that your saved by His grace, then right now is the time. The Word of God says: "If today you hear His voice harden not your heart". Those words were straight from God who is in Heaven, who also loves you and knows what is best for you.

You can know that you know, by admitting you're a sinner and turning from your sin. This is illustrated like releasing the baggage, like releasing your grip on those things that God calls sin. This happens as you come to Him with all of your sins, you come just as you are right now sins and all and agreeing with Him that you're a sinner. "All have sinned and fall short of the glory of God" (Romans 3:23). That's you, me and everyone else in this world. But there is hope!

Now that we see that we are all sinners, we also see in God's scripture that, "The wages of sin is death, but the free gift of God is eternal life in Christ Jesus our Lord" (Romans 6:23).

When you open the door and allow Jesus in then this very scripture will become true for you: "Therefor there is now no condemnation for those who are in Christ Jesus" (Romans 8:1)

Now the big moment of truth. You must say it with your mouth from your heart with words. This is what God's word says: But what does it say "THE WORD IS NEAR YOU, IN YOUR MOUTH AND IN YOUR HEART" – that is, the word of faith which we are preaching, that if you confess with your mouth Jesus as Lord, and believe in your heart that God raised Him from the dead, you will be saved" (Romans 10:8-10).

So now pray this prayer out loud with your mouth and from your heart: "Lord I give you my life. I am a sinner and I know it. Please forgive me. I believe in Jesus Christ. I believe He died on the cross. I believe He shed His blood for me. I believe He rose from the grave. I believe He is alive right now. So, I give you my life. You are my savior and my Lord. I trust in You as my Lord. Please fill me with your Holy Spirit and help me to live for You every single day. In Jesus name I pray. Amen."

If you just prayed that prayer and meant it, you are now a child of God, with His love and Spirit living inside of you. So, congratulations, you are now in the family of God.

Make sure you read the Bible, pray, and fellowship with other believers. So make sure you go to a loving, Bible teaching and believing church.

This is the best news for you. How awesome is our God? Thank God that He is in the "Saving" business. Thank God that He never changes. He's the same yesterday, and forever.

And our blessed assurance is, He's…

The Same Today

ABOUT THE AUTHOR

George was born in Santa Cruz, California and raised by a loving mother and father who are followers Jesus. They taught him the Bible from his earliest years. He was raised in a large ministry that helped people right off of the street with drug problems. His family became an outreach in Albuquerque, New Mexico in 1979. He was 9 years old when they moved there and was starting to get into a lot of trouble.

He attended Calvary Albuquerque when it started in 1982. It was during that time that "Seeds" were being planted in his heart by hearing the Word of God taught by Pastor Skip Heitzig.

It was a year later in Tucson, Arizona that he gave his life to Jesus and was "Born Again".

His family moved back to Santa Cruz when he was 14 and he became an avid surfer. Surfing became his life and slowly he drifted away from close relationship with Jesus.

At twenty-one years old he knew that living to surf was a

dead end. So he volunteered to become an Army Ranger. During this time in the Rangers he learned how to be a man. Though he learned much he was still a lost son to God. The party life was everything until he met the love of his life, Christina. Later they married and they moved back to his home town of Santa Cruz.

His wife, work and surfing was his priority until they had their first child in 2002. Later they decided that it would be better to raise their son in Washington State. He started to go to church again and turn back toward the Lord.

It was a men's conference at Calvary Fellowship in Seattle that he re-committed his life to Jesus. Greg Laurie was preaching and he felt the touch in his heart of the Holy Spirit to stand up for the prayer of re-dedication to Jesus.

Since that time he began to teach and preach at his Church and many of these Sunday sermons and Wednesday night teachings became books as well.

GEORGE CRABB

The Same Today

Other books by the Author available at:

Amazon books   Barnes & Noble   Apple ibooks

Road to Emmaus

George Crabb

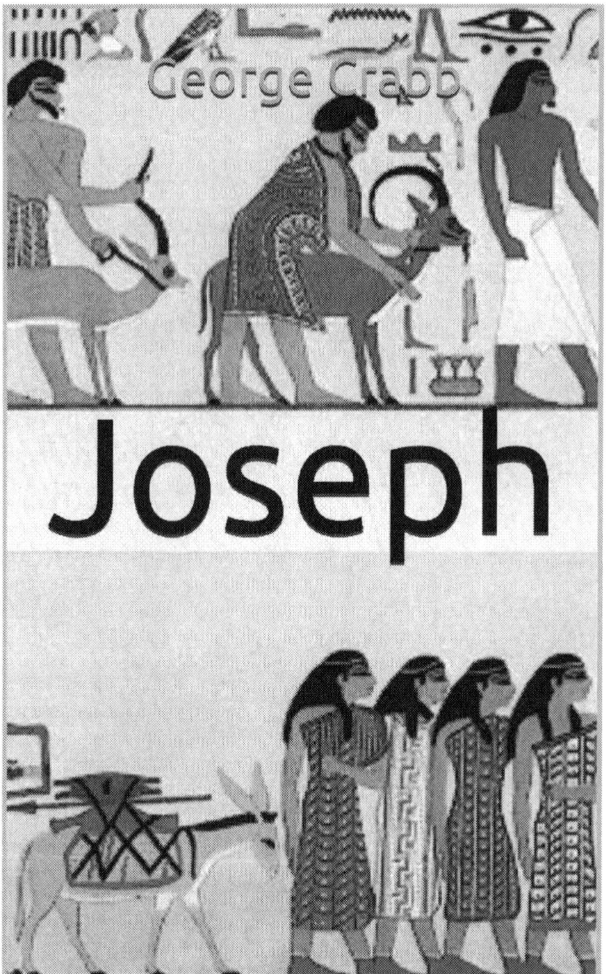
George Crabb
Joseph

BETHLEHEM EPHRATHAH

GEORGE CRABB

Made in the USA
Charleston, SC
19 August 2016